THE
BICYCLE
BOOK

B
R

THE BICYCLE BOOK

In association with

CYCLING PLUS

WEIDENFELD & NICOLSON

Contents

4 Cycling safety

5 Riding for life

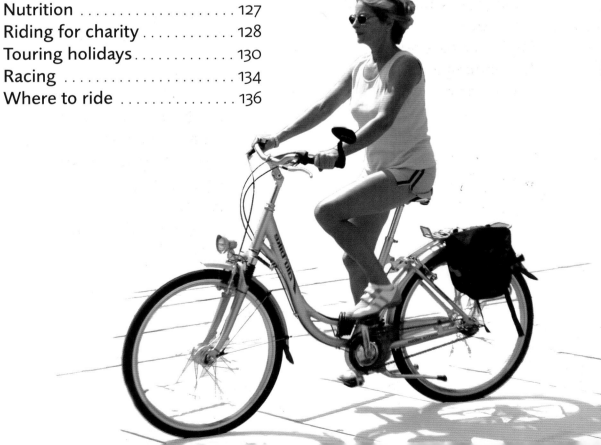

Saddle up for the best cycling advice...

The best thing about cycling is that while it feels like too much fun to be good for you, it actually is – ride a bike regularly and you'll be lighter, healthier, you will live longer and it will even save you money. For a start, cycling is an extremely **healthy activity**, giving you a good cardiovascular workout without stressing your joints. Riding a bike is also a great way of **losing weight** and then keeping it off – if you want to shed the pounds then just take to your bike and you won't need to go on a diet. It takes years off you, too. Regular cyclists have been proven to not only **live longer** but to be both mentally and physically more active and alert further into old age.

But cycling offers you more than just health benefits. In many cities a bike is now easily the **quickest** and least stressful way of getting around town as you are unlikely to get caught up in traffic jams. Plus, if you ride in central London not only will you save on bus and tube fares but you won't have to pay the congestion charge either (Londoners just saving on the congestion charge would be around £1,000 a year better off). If you're switching from car, train, bus or tube you could save a great deal and your **new bike will pay for itself** in no time – after that it's money in the bank. The bonus is you'll be getting fitter, too – so you can save on those gym fees as well.

Of course, the best reason for riding a bike is that it's just such a **fantastically enjoyable** thing to do. Britain has a wealth of scenic backwaters and quiet byways, which are best explored on two wheels, while America has the 53,000-km (33,000-mile) National Bicycle Route Network as well as many **quiet and beautiful trails**. With the continued growth of the National Cycle Network, the National Byway, Sustrans, and loads of urban cycle paths and corridors out into the countryside in Britain, there are now thousands of miles of safe routes suitable for every type of cyclist, young or old. On top of that there are tens of thousands of miles of quiet roads, plus a similar mileage of off-road bridleways and byways plus an increasing number of purpose-built forest trails, all of which are best seen from the saddle of a bike. A bike gives you the **freedom to explore** and experience your environment in a way you never can by car, and to really get off the beaten track.

Cycling offers **something for everyone**, whether you are looking for a quicker and less stressful way to get to work, a new hobby to enjoy with your family, or you want to exercise your competitive streak with time trials or events. Instead of dragging yourself to the gym to work out on the treadmill why not grab your bike and reinvigorate yourself with an hour's cycling around your city or out in the countryside; or encourage your children to have a more active lifestyle by planning fun days out by bike. Include a stop at a playground or a picnic in a woodland clearing and your children will be clamouring for you to take them out again. Added to this there are numerous charity rides, races and club events just waiting for you to try them out.

As everyone deserves the chance to find out for themselves how much life on two wheels has to offer we have put together this book. We will give you all the information you need to **find the right bike** for your needs, **at the best price**, as well as the **clothes** and **accessories** you will require, from seasonal clothing to helmets, lights and locks. And we are not stopping there. Because we are also going to show you how to get the most from your new purchase with expert advice on **riding technique**, **safety** and health as well as suggestions on how to find great places to ride. Believe us, once you get started with the right bike and kit you won't ever want to stop...

Commuting by bike

Save money, save time, get fit – there's no end to the benefits of commuting by bike.

If you cycle to work you can have your cake and eat it. Your ride in lets you arrive at the office on time, fired up and ready to go instead of late, half-asleep and stressed. And you can enjoy a guilt-free slab of actual cake when you get there: moderate cycling burns 300 calories an hour, so a 30-minute each way commute equals a cake a day – or a yearly loss of 10kg (1^1/$_2$ stone) of body fat (77,000 calories!) if you're dieting. More cycling, more cake – and no catch: that's commuting. No wonder cycle-commuters are the happiest, healthiest workers and take the least time off sick.

Avoiding the daily grind

Getting to work is a bore for most commuters. Cyclists have it easier because train strikes and traffic jams won't slow you down. On your journey to work you will be able to maintain a fairly constant average speed. After a few attempts you will know your commuting time to the minute (great for training), and if you're running late you can just pedal harder.

Weather is an issue for cyclists, but in many countries the odds of rain falling on you while you are actually commuting are slim. Even in Britain you ought not to get rained on heavily more than a dozen times a year. Wind is a bigger annoyance. While good clothing, lower gears and a philosophical outlook will minimize your irritation, why not just leave the bike at home on days with inclement weather? It is not written that you must ride every day – if you only cycle half the year, you'll still rack up half the savings and half the health benefits.

What you need

It really doesn't matter what type of bike you ride, you can still use it to commute. From folders, hack bikes, hybrids, mountain bikes and tourers to commuter specials – and all points in between – virtually all bikes make suitable commuting machines. You also don't need a lot of special gear or equipment – just make sure that you have good lights (see page 52), a high-quality lock (or locks) (see page 54), weatherproof clothing (see page 72) and a good pannier (see page 66) for carrying your kit, then add what you need depending on the length and type of commute you do (see page 10).

Being presentable

People often walk to the office in smart clothes, but they don't run to work in a suit. This is a useful parallel when cycling. If you're going to wear the clothes you cycled in at work then you mustn't race and get sweaty. Resist that inner demon that tells you to ride faster, especially when another cyclist comes past you. Keep your cool. If you get hot, stop and shed a layer. Also avoid carrying things on your back.

If you're getting changed when you get to work, you can ride how you wish. Clearly this approach works better if there's a shower at work, but as you won't be wearing your sweaty clothes, which are what trap bad scents, it's not vital. Have a face wash; a once-over with an unscented wet wipe; apply deodorant and, if relevant, make-up. Comb your hair and put on your office clothes – and the cyclist has disappeared!

Whether you're wearing normal clothes or bike clothes while cycling, the key is not to overheat. As with any cycling, this is usually a bigger problem than getting too cold.

Finally, don't go to the trouble of looking smart, then ruin it by pulling out a bright yellow pannier full of dog-eared files. A good-sized courier bag will hold a normal briefcase inside, or you can get a shoulder bag that looks the business by itself. Briefcase-style panniers are available that mount to the rear rack at an angle to clear your heel; these are great for paperwork, but while they will accommodate your laptop computer, it is inadvisable to carry your computer in it as it will be subject to vibration and may break.

Advice for different commutes

Here are four different commuting scenarios along with what we reckon are the optimum bikes, modifications and accessories for the job. That said, we can't stress highly enough that you can do almost any commute on almost any bike.

Short-distance commuting: No sweat

For a commute of this kind – up to 6½km (4 miles) on streetlit, urban roads – you can ride literally anything from a top-end race bike to any old rustbucket. As less time is spent cycling – 5km (3 miles) takes around 15 minutes at a medium pace – you can best improve your journey times by minimizing the non-cycling element of your journey. If you can walk out of the door, get on the bike and go at a moment's notice, you could be halfway there while the racer is still looking for his cycling shoes.

Bike: All you really need is a bike with an upright riding position for excellent visibility, a wider saddle because that's where your weight will be, 35mm or 37mm tyres for comfort, a hub gear, full mudguards and a chain guard. You could also try a decent 700c wheeled hybrid, which is widely available and also offers an upright comfortable ride; and most common of all, the mountain bike – even if it's never used off-road. Though do put on a set of slick or semi-slick tyres to improve on-road riding performance.

Accessories: A kickstand is great if you're on and off your bike a lot. An immobilizer is useful when dashing into shops, though irrelevant for point-to-point commuting – take a better lock too (see page 54). On streetlit roads, lighting means 'being seen', so make sure your lights are both bright and long-lasting (see page 52). Whatever lights you use, have a back-up front and rear light.

Clothing: If you're not riding at pace you can wear anything, particularly on a roadster. That's the point. Just avoid thick seams, which you get in jeans, or very long coats or scarves. And don't dress too warmly. It's best to wear layers so you can take one off at a time if you get too hot.

Lights on your bike allow you to see and be seen – battery powered (pictured), or by dynamo. Locks are also vital for city commuters and are often inexpensive. Opposite, a saddle bag big enough for documents and clothing. See page 140

Medium-distance commuting:
Pre-work warm-up

At a distance of 6–16km (4–10 miles), the more upright riding position of a roadster becomes a chore: it's slow and you may get a sore bottom. The argument for wearing dedicated cycling clothes, at least in winter, is a lot stronger.

Bike: Basic touring bikes will serve, as will hybrids. There is also a legion of 26in mountain bikes, which you can modify to a greater or lesser extent. If you want to go further down the custom route, On-One, Caribou and Thorn all do frames suited to building fast, rugged 26in wheel commuters.

Accessories: Proper lighting is essential (see page 52). Even if you're carrying some gear in a courier bag, a rear rack with a pannier or bag lets you divide your load, putting the heavier stuff on the bike (see page 66).

Clothing: It depends how hard you ride and what's acceptable dress at work. In winter, you can wear cycling tights along with winter boots on your bottom half, and just throw a cycling jacket over your work shirt. Then you've only got to change your trousers. In summer, most casual shorts are fine for cycling; add knee warmers for cool spring or late-summer starts. If you're carrying weight on your back, padded cycling shorts will prevent the saddle pressing uncomfortably. Get a gilet (or vest) to keep the wind off without stifling you. Combined with arm warmers, you'll be fine for most dry weather conditions. Take a nylon rain cape or lightweight jacket for showers (see also pages 72–81).

Long-distance commuting: Mile eating

We're defining this as 16km (10 miles) or more each way, and some of it will probably be on rural roads. A moderately fit rider can manage this day in, day out. Yet it's still a chunk of time to spend cycling; the ride home can seem to take for ever. Minimize your effort and riding time by cycling quickly.

Bike: 26in wheel bikes with slicks are still viable at this distance, as are tourers – particularly shod with the right tyres. Drop bars or tribars, which you can fit to flat bars, let you pile on the speed and are good in the wind. Old road frames with forward-facing dropouts are a budget option. Touring or cyclo-cross style road frames with forward-facing dropouts are better still: you'll have clearance for 28mm+ tyres and bosses for cantilever brakes.

And though most of us will ride with derailleurs, hard-core riders can run a fixed gear; slightly less hard-core riders a singlespeed; and soft core riders a hub gear. As you're riding fast and hard, give yourself a higher top gear: 53in, 70in and a 93in 'overdrive', perhaps.

Accessories: Good lights, as for medium-distance commuting (see page 52). To ride faster, minimize what you're carrying. Buy two locks and leave one at work. Leave your shoes and jacket at work, and take your trousers and five shirts in at the start of the week. On an upright roadster, bags and rucksacks hang comfortably from your shoulders; bent over, your back takes the strain. To avoid this choose panniers that can be fitted even to bikes that won't take racks (see also page 66).

Clothing: Full bike kit is best, whether in summer or winter (see pages 72–81).

Mixed mode commuting: Flexible working

This can mean two things: you can ride to work some days and not others; or you can combine cycling with another form of transport on the same day. For example, bike and train.

Bike: One bike goes on trains better than any other because it packs so small: the Brompton. On certain train lines you don't even need a folder – you can put your full-size bike on the train without booking, and without fear that there won't be room (check with your train network). If you do the same train journey all the time, you can leave a cheap hack locked up at the station near where you work.

Accessories: Black Brompton front pannier bags are smart enough to serve as briefcases.

Clothing: As with roadsters, you should be able to wear your work clothes on a folder – as long as you have trouser clips.

Top tips for commuting

1 How to avoid falling off

Obviously you have to keep an eye out for errant drivers, other cyclists, pedestrians and dogs. But there are problems that are harder to spot. Drain covers and slick tarmac 'sealing lines' are lethal when wet or oily: if you can't avoid riding on them, be sure you're going in a straight line with your bike fully upright. Black ice is worse still, since you can't see it. All you can do is remember where you hit a patch and avoid that place in future when it's frosty; it often re-occurs in the same location.

2 What to do if you're ill

Stay at home and get better. Most short to medium commutes aren't that hard, so if you're too ill to ride your bike you're probably too ill to be at work. If you absolutely have to get there, use a different form of transport. If you force your body to ride, it may reward you with fainting or dizzy spells at the journey's end.

3 How to avoid stress

Cyclists have more predictable journey times than drivers, so rushing is rarely a problem. The big stress factor on a bike is aggressive language or behaviour from other road users or pedestrians. Getting into an argument may let you blow off steam, but rarely does any good. Better to rise above it.

4 How to deal with oil

Cycle clips and trouser bands are okay, but if you're wearing your best trousers you'll somehow still get oil on them. Gaiters or even leg warmers will keep trouser bottoms cleaner. If you get oily hands then a palm full of sugar and washing-up liquid should get your hands presentable.

5 How to carry your laptop

On your back, in a 100 per cent waterproof courier bag. If you carry the laptop in a rack-mounted pannier, then the computer will be subject to a lot of vibration, which could shorten its life expectancy or even break it.

6 Why to avoid mountain bike mudguards

They don't work. Partial mudguards give partial protection. Down-tube guards are fine for deflecting clods of mud but do little to keep road spray off you. To keep yourself clean, use full mudguards – with a mudflap for the front mudguard if you want to keep your feet dry as well. See also page 58.

Cycling for the family

When the sun is shining there is no better day out with the kids than a bike ride, and it's healthy too.

Children love cycling. It's time spent with you, talking together, discovering things and enjoying fresh air and exercise. Children pick up on your enthusiasm, and as they get older, a bicycle is their independence.

Family cycling isn't only about introducing your children to two wheels. Often it's a time when a non-cycling partner starts riding again. If one of you is already an experienced cyclist buy your other half a reasonable bike – one of a quality you'd consider for yourself, even if it's different from the kind of bike you'd choose. Depending on the type of riding you and, more importantly, your partner intend to do, you won't go wrong with one of the many types of hybrid bikes. Unless your partner really intends to seriously off-road a hybrid is probably a better bet than a mountain bike because it is more than capable of dealing with whatever you are likely to throw at it.

Let your partner set the pace and the mileage, and level the playing field by fitting the trailer, child seat or luggage to your bike. Stay away from busy roads, which are intimidating and prevent conversation. And relax! If nobody is enjoying it, you're doing it wrong.

Younger non-bike-riding children

Up until the age of four or five, small children are non-pedalling passengers. Fortunately, with the right equipment such as a child seat, trailer bike or trailer and a helmet they're fairly portable (see page 62).

The hardest part of cycling with small children is getting out of the door. It's like an expedition. Try to minimize morning prep time. The night before, check bikes and equipment, make the packed lunch, lay out clothes, prepare a pannier or seat pack with tools, first aid kit, etc.

With a trailer or seat, as your child is under your direct control, you can ride anywhere. Busy roads aren't any more dangerous, though conversation is impossible. Lanes are better, while both tandems and trailer bikes will go off-road, making single tracks, bridleways and forest tracks all possible.

Most trailers can be stored easily and are suitable for children between nine months and nine years old. Some can also be converted to strollers, as pictured. See page 140

At this age children don't need much entertaining, although they will want to stretch their legs. Aim for somewhere with a bit of grass or a play area. Keep mileages low and take plenty of snacks and drinks. Local lanes and Sustrans paths are ideal routes (see page 136). On longer rides you need to check their morale and energy levels regularly, and if necessary boost both with stops and snacks. Adults can feel themselves getting tired; children can conk out in moments and suddenly be upset and tearful – or fast asleep.

To avoid accidents, it is vital that nothing – clothing, feet, fingers – can end up in a wheel. All trailers have side panels to prevent this, and most child seats have foot straps and side panels. Dangling laces, scarves or mittens-on-strings can still be a risk. Make sure, too, that you periodically check all your family's cycling equipment for loose screws, unsafe bolts, etc.

In the summer avoid sunburn by liberally applying factor 30 and/or choosing light clothing with arm and leg coverage. The back of the neck is particularly vulnerable for children slumped in child seats. Dress your child with an extra layer of clothing as he or she won't get as hot as you.

In the winter children can – and do – get very cold, even in trailers. Wrap them up really well. Ski-style salopettes make great overtrousers. A balaclava under the helmet (remove some padding) will prevent painfully cold ears. Wellington boots are useful even in trailers, which may collect water in the footwell in torrential rain.

Older bike-riding children

Children as young as six can ride 20km (12 miles), and by the age of ten or eleven most are keen to use their own bikes. Independent cycling offers a wonderful sense of freedom and achievement.

When your child is old enough to have their own bike, don't be tempted to buy a bike that your child will 'grow into'. An over-large bike will be awkward to ride. As a rule of thumb, 14in or 16in wheel bikes suit ages four to six; 20in ages five to ten; and 24in ages eight to twelve.

The snag can be finding a suitable bike as most children's bikes are underspecced and overweight and can be up to half the rider's total bodyweight! Your child will get more out of cycling with a lighter bike. Aim for 13kg (2 stone) or less for 20in and 24in wheel bikes, especially if they're likely to go off-road. A long seatpost and a steerer with plenty of spacer washers – or a quill stem – will maximize growing room. Children often prefer a seat height that's lower than optimum, and anyway they must be able to stand over the bike and dab a foot when seated. Brakes also need to be reachable by smaller hands.

The number of gears is a badge of status among children, but in fact, too many gears cause mechanical complications. One gear is best for starter bikes, a 3-speed hub for second bikes, and a 7- or 8-speed derailleur for pre-teens. Most children's bikes have Gripshift, which is a good thing as it doesn't need much hand-strength to use.

Trailer bikes that can fold up like this one are ideal for days out and the school run. See page 140

A helmet (see page 65) is an obvious precaution, and cycling mitts can help prevent scuffed hands. Long trousers such as tracksuit bottoms and shirts with sleeves are better than bare arms and legs. They offer protection from minor grazes, scratches and nettle stings. Boots or sturdy trainers are better than sandals or plimsoles for the same reason.

Off-road areas are ideal for children to develop bike-handling skills, and to enjoy it while doing so. Lack of traffic means you can talk more easily, and the riding can be technically interesting. Sooner or later your child will fall off off-road, but falls at this age are rarely serious because there's no traffic or street furniture to hit, and speeds are generally low. (It's worth carrying some plasters though...)

As always, plan the ride so you're going to places that will interest the children – a café stop here, a good place for trying to do jumps there, whatever interests them. Don't overestimate your speed or how far you will be able to travel when planning the route. If they're on their own bikes, you may be averaging only 8km/h (5mph) or so off-road.

Comfort

- Buy an inflatable neck cushion – smaller children require full back and head support as when they start to nod off, they'll literally do that in their seat.
- Children in seats are susceptible to cold and rain. Make sure they are wearing a number of warm layers. Canoe spraydeck-style capes that go over the seat and your child (but leave the head poking out) are ideal for rainy weather.
- An adult's cotton cycling cap will fit a child under a helmet, and worn back to front will protect the neck from sunburn.
- Flies and other insects can freak out small children, who often attract them by being sticky, so consider some kind of repellent, or ride where insects won't be.
- Any seat upholstery should be removable so it can be washed.

Go touring

If you can ride a bike to the shops, you can ride it across counties, countries or even continents.

Anyone can tour by bicycle. There's no minimum or maximum speed, duration or distance; no age limit; no particular abilities or equipment required; and no rules. All you need is a bike and the desire to travel (see also pages 130–133).

Not so fast

Bombing down dual carriageways is for time triallists or motorists. Touring is best on minor roads the smaller the better. Since the shortest point between two places will often be linked by the biggest road, this will mean taking a more roundabout route. But that's the essence of touring: enjoying the journey, not minimizing the journey time. It's not that minor roads are more scenic – though they often are – it's that they carry less traffic.

Busy roads make touring like commuting, and even an hour spent on one can spoil your whole day. If there's no suitable lane, what about a bridleway or canal towpath? If you're deliberately not getting there the fastest way you can, it makes no sense to use the fastest bike either. Wider tyres offer greater shock absorption and won't pinch flat under loads. A more upright riding position reduces strain on your back, shoulders and hands – and it lets you look at your surroundings instead of down at the tarmac. Plus you may want a different saddle, given that more of your weight will be resting on it. As for gears, it doesn't matter how many you've got as long as they go low enough for you.

A cycle tour offers the perfect opportunity to explore some of Britain's most unspoilt regions, from National Parks, to lakes and moorlands. Touring is a chance to get out of the towns and cities and you're in charge. Don't be put off by the fact that the most famously gruelling cycle race in the world is, perhaps disingenuously, known as the Tour de France; a cycle tour can be tailored to suit everyone. As long as you have checked your equipment thoroughly, set yourself realistic targets in terms of distance and difficulty, and are prepared for inclement weather touring can be one of the most enjoyable ways to cycle.

How to enjoy your tour

- Don't forget to have a 'shakedown tour'. This is a weekend (or longer) trial run. Load your bike up with everything you intend to take, then do the daily mileage you intend to do on your trip, preferably on similar terrain.
- Do use your shakedown tour to add to or subtract from your kit list.
- Give yourself plenty of time to fix the bike up right before you go.
- Don't accept any advice that makes you uncomfortable on your bike. What works for others may not work for you.
- Do include 'rest days' off the bike, especially if you're covering a large distance.
- Don't forget travel insurance.
- Do head for the launderette if you get soaked!
- Don't try anything brand new – especially a saddle or pair of shoes – at the start of a tour.
- Do use Loctite or similar to secure pannier rack bolts in place.
- Don't overlook group tours. It's a different experience entirely, and worth trying.

Touring essentials

A few simple tools – a multi-tool kit, pump, tyre levers and patches, for example (see pages 60 and 86) – and the knowledge to use them are recommended. Learning maintenance is much easier if you're shown, so why not enrol in a cycle maintenance class before you go (see page 98). Since you can't prepare for all eventualities, you should also have enough money (or a credit card) to get you home by other means. Personal identification may not be needed often but is worth carrying (if you're in an accident, for example). On any but the shortest rides, take a showerproof jacket; you can get cold very quickly when you get wet.

Likewise, always take at least one water bottle plus a high energy snack, like an energy bar or flapjack. Hunger knock ('the bonk') is a sudden empty-tank feeling of utter weakness that has to be felt to be believed. Avoid it. Front and rear lights are essential, even if you're planning to ride only in daytime, as you could get delayed. A good bar bag is handy so you can keep snacks, camera, a first aid kit, mobile phone, etc., in there and you don't need to stop to get anything out of it. A map trap is also very useful on any ride. Lastly, take at least a dozen zip ties. Loose mudguards and racks are just the start of the long list of things these can fix.

Preparing for your tour

If you have a reasonable base level of fitness from commuting or racing, you don't need to worry about training. Just don't

Be sure to take everything needed: multi-tools and the correct size bag and rack to accommodate all that you carry. See page 140

over-commit yourself for your first few days. This is doubly important if you don't have that fitness base. A cycling newbie can ride 96–115km (60–70 miles) in a day, but will struggle to do any distance at all the day after. Otherwise, let your fitness build as you go. If you've overestimated your daily mileage – as a rule of thumb, don't ride more than two-thirds of the distance that you could do as a one off, under the same conditions – reschedule your plans.

Whether you plan everything in advance or make it up as you go is your choice; most people will find a reasonable compromise somewhere between these extremes. The more you're prepared to spend and the more self-sufficient you are, the more flexible you can be.

Researching your route and accommodation is easily undertaken on the internet; when you've narrowed things down, a good guide book will tell you what you have to know, even if most aren't aimed specifically at cyclists.

If you've never toured before, then the easiest place to start is your back door. Pick a destination about 30–50km (20–30 miles) away, ride there on the smallest roads you can find, stay overnight, and then come home. After that you can try something a little more ambitious, like the Coast to Coast in Britain, a weekend in Ireland or a road trip in America. Book a week off work – now – and get planning!

Customizing your bike for touring

Fortunately, you don't have to splash out on a specialist touring bike. If you don't have a tourer, here's how to make your bike more suitable for touring (see also page 89).

Road bike

Fine for shorter tours. Load limits are restricted by 32-hole rims, narrow tyres, a double-chainring and the (in)ability to fit racks. You'll make life a lot easier for yourself if you fit a triple chainset, removing the outer ring if you want to retain your short arm rear mech. Get hold of some wider tyres. Light loads can go on a rear rack or you can use Carradice Limpet front panniers. Don't overload the rear wheel. You can also use saddlebags or bar bags.

Mountain Bike

Mudguard and rack eyes have all but disappeared from almost all new mountain bikes except customized ones. You can get round this by buying a second-hand mountain bike instead, or you could carry your luggage in Carradice Limpets, a saddlebag or a trailer or by using 'P' clips. Fit handlebar ends and touring tyres.

Hybrids

Get one with rack eyes, the space for wider (up to 37mm) tyres, and cantilever or V-brakes. If you've got what is essentially a flat-barred road bike, follow advice for road bikes – and fit handlebar ends.

Folder

Not as daft as it sounds. You can comfortably do 80km (50 miles) on a Brompton or Birdy, and you can take your bike on a train or into your hotel room. Fit stubby handlebar ends and use good tyres. If using a 3-speed bike, get a larger sprocket fitted.

Go racing

Anyone can race, so if you fancy a new challenge then why not look into road racing or track racing?

Road racing

Why do people want to road race? To invigorate an increasingly suppressed fighting gene? To get away from her/him indoors? To avoid doing time trials? There are all sorts of reasons. Some of these might include the development of tactics, fitness, camaraderie and competition. And then there's also the love of cycling itself – riding a top-end race bike and emulating your Tour de France hero will give you a real buzz.

If you fancy trying a different way of cycling then why not consider road racing? (see also pages 134–135.) Most road racing is carried out on the open roads, but there are also a growing number of races run on closed circuits. If you are new to road racing then it's probably best to join a club, as most automatically affiliate themselves to the necessary bodies and have a club strip. Most clubs should either have a coach or at least a few experienced members who don't mind advising on training, racing, etc.

Racing bike

You don't need to spend a lot to be competitive, but obviously you need to have at least an entry-level bike and some rudimentary kit in order to race. Unless you are super-human, a mountain bike with slicks probably won't cope. Budget on spending around £400 to £500 minimum if you are buying new and £300 second-hand. If you do buy second-hand make sure you know what size you should be looking for.

Because a road bike is designed to climb, sprint and time trial, anything is suitable as long as it is reasonably light – under $10^{1}/_{2}$kg (23lb). It is not important to have aerodynamic wheels although they do need to be well-tensioned and reasonably light. The bike has to be safe, and although scrutineering is a thing of the past, the commissaire (referee) or other competitors may point out any defect.

You will need a double chainring with a good spread of medium to high gears. Something like a 52 or 53 big chainring and a 42 or 39 inner coupled to a 12- to 23- or 26-tooth set of sprockets will suit most courses.

Wearing the right kit

Your racing kit will need to be able to cope with a variety of conditions – in very cold weather, a training jacket or long-sleeved top will be necessary and this is best worn over a sweat-wicking undervest or T-shirt. Cold and wet early season races require a set of long, or 3/4 length, tights. Alternatively, knee and arm warmers are very useful because they can be rolled down or removed once you, or the weather, have warmed up. In hot weather, you need to wear the minimum short-sleeved jersey and knee-length shorts to conform to general appearance standards (see also pages 72–81).

Always wear trackmitts or gloves in case of a spill. It is obligatory to wear an approved crash hat, and make sure that you replace your crash helmet if it has previously taken any significant blows.

If you use a pulsemeter, wear it passively and don't assume that you will be in a position to control your pulse, especially up hills when the pack tends to go as hard as it can.

Track racing

Track racing is an addictive high-adrenaline experience, but it's got much more to offer than just thrills. It is a great thing to do as it sharpens your bike handling, provides a great workout and gets the adrenaline flowing like nothing else. If you have a go, you won't stop talking about it for weeks.

The track racing community is relatively small, so there's a chance that if you do go into track racing with the aim of competing seriously, you could do relatively well in a short space of time. Of course, it's highly unlikely that you'll come close to matching the amazing progress of Jason Queally, who only took up the sport in 1995, suffered a major injury shortly afterwards, but still competed in the 1998 Commonwealth Games in Kuala Lumpur where he won a Silver medal and, of course, went on to win Gold in the 2000 Olympics in Sydney.

There are many different kinds of track racing event from all-out sprints to more tactical team events, but once you find your ideal discipline (see also pages 134–5), the chances are you'll be hooked – and you'll see your general handling and bike skills improve dramatically thanks to the demands of track racing.

The bike

You will need a fixed-wheel bike (this is radically different to a road bike). These start at about £150 for an old second-hand model, or about £650 for a new one.

Although there are no ballistic descents, average speeds on the velodrome are high, so the bikes have to be both responsive and stable, quick to steer but predictable and, most importantly, dependable.

Starting out

First off, it's not a bad idea to have a go at riding a fixed-wheel bike before you get to a track. When you first have a go, try to find a flat, empty car park so that you can get used to starting and stopping. Remember that you cannot stop pedalling around corners so don't get too cocky. Try slowing down without using your brakes and practise standing up, out of the saddle.

Next find a track near you and go and watch some of the different kinds of races that take place there. Talk to other track racers and get a feel for what level or kind of race you wish to take part in.(see also pages 134–5).

Some dos and don'ts of racing

- Do learn to ride steadily in the bunch. By watching what everyone else is doing and by emulating the experienced riders, you will soon mesh in with the group and present no danger. Spin gears smoothly and stay on top of them, without lugging, up hills.
- Don't make sudden movements without checking around you first. This is done by a glance over both shoulders. Causing a crash on your first outing won't do much for your confidence or popularity within the peleton (the mass of moving cyclists).
- Do learn to anticipate the acceleration or deceleration within the peleton. This will save you plenty of energy and make you much safer within the pack.
- Don't try to overtake when you're riding into a sharp corner. The rider in front has priority and is not going to make considerations for your invisible move.
- Do sprint in a straight line. Swerving or 'switching', as it is known, is not only dangerous but can get you disqualified.
- Don't argue with the judges until you have done their job for many years. Contrary to your own opinion, they are the experts and should be respected.
- Do offer to help out with marshalling or administration tasks. Almost every race is run by volunteers, who would no doubt appreciate a helping hand.

Which bike is for you?

**The secret to enjoying cycling is to get the right bike for you –
one that suits your lifestyle and your physique.**

Some bikes are designed specifically for certain uses such as racing, while others are more adaptable to multiple uses. Depending on whether you want a bike that you can go off-road with, one for commuting a couple of kilometres/miles to work every day, or something that you take out occasionally at the weekend with your family, there is a bike out there to suit you.

Road bike

If speed is your thing then this is the bike for you. Light and nimble, the whole emphasis is on speed. Tyres are narrow and slick for lower rolling resistance and the 700c wheels are slightly larger than those on a mountain bike, which means that once up to speed these bikes are real mile eaters. However, they can be more prone to punctures and may not be as comfortable as a hybrid for everyday journeys. From about £400 up you will get integrated brake and gear levers.
IDEAL FOR: racing, time trials, fast fitness riding.
EXPECT TO PAY: £300–infinity.

Street bike

A fast-evolving new breed of bike. In its purest form it's basically a road bike with flat bars so you get the speed of a road bike with the riding position of a mountain bike. This makes them ideal fast commuting bikes, and some newer designs acknowledge this with tougher wheels than standard road bikes and greater tyre clearance so you can fit mudguards; some even take disc brakes.
IDEAL FOR: fast commuting, leisure and fitness riding, day touring.
EXPECT TO PAY: £350–£1,500.

Mountain bike

Get off the beaten track on a 'hardtail' mountain bike – a rigid frame with a suspension fork. Its 26in wheels are slightly smaller than a road bike's and they're much thicker too which makes for strength, comfort and acceleration. Originally designed for off-roading, the good manoeuvrability and suspension make these popular with commuters. Most hardtails will take racks or child seats. The knobbly tyres make pedalling harder so fit slick city tyres for road use. For more extreme off-roading go for a full suspension bike starting at around £500.

IDEAL FOR: off-road, leisure rides, commuting, touring, can be modified to do almost anything.
EXPECT TO PAY: £170–£5,000.

Hybrid bike

The classic hybrid is exactly as the name suggests: a hybrid of a road bike and a mountain bike with road sized 700c wheels mated to a mountain bike-style frame with flat bars for a more comfortable riding position so you get something of the speed of a road bike with the rugged durability of a mountain bike. These days there is a wide range of hybrids, some with a greater emphasis on comfort and some built more for speed.

IDEAL FOR: leisure rides, commuting, touring, or even popping down to the shops.
EXPECT TO PAY: £200–£800.

City bike

Stripped-down mountain bikes for city streets – some are fitted with low-maintenance hub gears. Their strong wheels and frame will take serious abuse, while wide slicks add comfort. Some models also have front suspension. Racks or child seats can be fitted; change the tyres for off-road use.

IDEAL FOR: commuting, leisure.
EXPECT TO PAY: £250–£500.

Touring bike

Long-distance load luggers built for comfort and strength. Make great commuting bikes and are versatile enough to be stripped down for time trialling, or taken off-road. Choose from 26in and 700c wheeled versions. Most tourers now come with a choice of drop or flat bars too. Racks and mudguards are usually standard as well.

IDEAL FOR: touring, leisure rides, commuting, like the mountain bike this is a great all-rounder.
EXPECT TO PAY: £500–£1,500.

Folding bike

Small is beautiful, particularly if you need a bike you can take on a bus or train, or stick in the boot of your car and take out to nail short-haul commutes. Some fold smaller and quicker than others. However, their small wheels and limited range of gears make them best for relatively short urban journeys only.

IDEAL FOR: commuting, or 'anything', say fans.

EXPECT TO PAY: £150–£1,500.

Recumbent bike

From the Latin 'recumbo' (to lie down), the rider doesn't step on the pedals from above but rests their body on a seat or hammock and pushes the drive with legs closer to the horizontal than the vertical. The distinctive look of these unusual bikes means you certainly won't go unnoticed in a recumbent!

IDEAL FOR: leisure rides, touring, even (recumbent) racing.

EXPECT TO PAY: £800–£1700.

Choosing the right bike for you

Riding a bike that doesn't fit is not only uncomfortable, but you risk injury from over-reaching, being too cramped, or because steering is compromised.

Having the right bike for you and having it correctly set up for your physique simply means that your bike fits you properly for the type(s) of riding you do. This could be for increased comfort, more speed or better aerodynamics. Getting the right fit means more than just having the right size bike – though that is important – it means that your bike fits you at all the main contact points: saddle, handlebars and pedals, so that you don't have to adopt an uncomfortable riding position.

Here we look at the ideal set-ups for general road riding, commuting/touring and time trialling, but of course we're not all the same, so use this information as a starting point. A good rule is that if it feels right it probably is... unless your body has become so used to a bad position that it has adapted to cope, but in that case you probably already have a bad back, dodgy knees and a stiff neck.

Buying the right size bike

Manufacturers make frames in various sizes to suit the variety of potential riders. Getting the size right is pretty crucial, but is only the first step. The fine-tuning occurs when you choose the length of the handlebar stem and the width of the handlebars. The fitting is completed by setting the handlebar and saddle height.

Decent cycle shops should help with all the steps for a perfect fit. They should get you on a fixed trainer bike so that your position can be checked once you're warmed up and riding in your normal shoes, pedals, shorts, etc.

Be prepared to stand back and view the bike. A correctly sized bike will look in proportion when finally set up. Compact frames are meant to look more radical than conventional level top tube frames so expect to see an extra 5–7cm (2–3in) of seat pin showing when compared to the older-style bikes. The contact points should be exactly the same, so be aware of this when buying – a compact should feel exactly like your favourite conventional road bike with respect to riding position.

Getting the right set-up

Step 1

Measure your standover height. The best way to do this is to stand over the bike with your bottom just touching the saddle as this should put you over the mid point of the top tube. Measure the gap between the top tube and your crotch. On a road bike there should be 5cm (2in) of standover height between your crotch and a horizontal top tube – 10cm (4in) on a mountain bike.

Step 2

Set your bike up horizontally on a fixed trainer and wear your normal cycling shoes and shorts. Measure your actual inside leg with socks on or to the top of the sole of your shoe at the heel. Do this by holding a level up in your crotch or just by pushing the end of the tape measure into your sit bone where you rest on the saddle...

Step 3

...Either way, make sure you get a realistic measurement of your inside leg and multiply this by 109 per cent to get your saddle top to pedal (at full extension in line with the seat tube) distance. This is a yardstick so be prepared to modify this by up to 15mm (1/2in) either side to compensate for different riding styles.

Set the saddle flat with scope to put the tip slightly up for men and slightly down for women. 'Slightly' means up to 8mm (1/4in) from the level. Set the saddle height to your 109 per cent in seam length, making sure there's at least 5cm (2in) of seatpost left in the seat tube – if there isn't you need a longer post or a taller bike.

Step 4

Get on and warm up enough so that you start pedalling naturally and then stop with your leg at full extension. Raise or lower the saddle until your leg becomes straight – don't try to stretch though. Your foot should be flat or slightly toe-down, but do make sure that you don't change your natural style for the set-up as things will immediately change when you get out on the road.

Once you're happy with the saddle height, concentrate on the reach to the handlebars – you don't want to be too cramped or too stretched. Start by positioning the saddle so that it's roughly halfway along the saddle rail. Rest your right elbow against the tip of the saddle with your left hand rested against the tips of your right fingers. Your left little finger should be in line with the middle of the handlebars. You should be relatively upright and comfortable. Similarly, you should be happy to spend lots of time on the brake hoods or tribars. Adjust the reach by either swapping the A-head stem for a shorter or longer one, or use an A-head adapter if your existing stem is a quill type.

2

3

Step 5

The drop portion of the handlebars should not be out of reach so spend time in this position to make sure that the brakes and gears are accessible. If they're not, take time to move the levers. A good starting point is to create a horizontal platform from the shoulders of the handlebars onto the hood of the brake levers. This provides a comfortable cruising position while still allowing access from the drops.

Riders with small hands can use handlebars that have reduced sections behind the shifters or a modified profile to allow easier access to the shift levers.

Step 6

Check the handlebar width by comparing the measurement across the shoulders with that across the handlebars, and be prepared to go wider or narrower accordingly. Remember that wide handlebars open the arms and have the effect of dragging you forward, which is not good news for smaller, slighter riders. Measure the handlebars across the centre of the ends – 38cm (15in) is narrow and 44cm (17in) wide.

Step 7

Dropping a plumb line from the kneecap will give you a rough idea of how evenly your weight is distributed, and will also give you a fix on your cleat position.

The plumb line should drop through the pedal spindle – if it doesn't, then move the saddle fore or aft to correct.

The ball of your foot should be over the pedal spindle for balanced pedalling. You may have a preference for lifting and dropping your heel when pedalling (called ankling) or you might prefer to push bigger gears with a stiffer ankle action. In the first instance move the cleats forwards for more ankle freedom and conversely for big gear crunching (not recommended if there's a choice).

1 Road bike

The dominant dimension on a road bike is the reach to the handlebars. The reference measurement from your frame is a horizontal line from the top of the centre of the head tube to the centre of the seat tube (or seat pin on compact frames). An average top tube will measure 55cm (21 ½in) with short and long ones measuring 53cm (21in) and 58cm (23in).

If you're between 160cm (5 feet 3 in) and 170cm (5 feet 7 in) you will need a frame with a 53cm or 54cm (21in) top tube. Riders between 172 cm (5 feet 8 in) and 180cm (5 feet 11 in) require 54cm (21in) to 56cm (22in) top tubes; and riders from 183cm (6 feet) to 193cm (6 feet 4 in) need 56cm (22in) to 58cm (23in) top tubes.

Getting the right fit at the contact points is the primary aim of a well set-up bike, but don't overlook a well-balanced set-up that produces good handling in all circumstances.

6

7

The frame's top tube, for example, should be coupled to a 9cm (3 ^{1}/$_2$in) to 13cm (5in) handlebar stem. Longer stems have more flex and make the handling less predictable, with a slower response than shorter stems, which are stiffer with a quick, direct response. Anything outside the normal risks upsetting the intended dynamics of the standard road frame.

Although the reach to the handlebars on a road bike is both forward and down, a correctly set-up road bike will enable the rider to reach all parts of the handlebars without any stress. You should reach the top of the handlebars with your arms not quite straight and your back at an angle of around 45 degrees. The reach to the hoods should be longer and lower but still comfortable for extended periods. The position on the drops should also be maintainable for long periods and comfortable on fast downhill sections where the rider prefers to get the strongest grip on the brakes. One of the most common errors when buying a road bike is to have the handlebars too long and too low, especially for women with a shorter torso. Remedying this situation can involve flipping the handlebar stem, so that it rises out of the headset, or shortening the reach by swapping to a smaller stem.

The fitting should all go on at the front end of the bike. The quick fix is to move the saddle forward or back to make up for a long or short reach, but this forces the rider away from the classic saddle to pedal position that gives choice between power or relaxation.

Last but not least, sort out your position on the pedals. It's important to get this one right as poorly positioned feet can lead to all sorts of problems from hot spots – where the pedal or cleat digs into your foot cutting off the circulation – to knee and leg problems (see also page 117). For performance riding there is an 'ideal' position (see step 6), but as with everything else here it's not set in stone and if things still aren't quite right don't be afraid to make minor adjustments. Remember, though, to keep each one small and to give yourself time to get used to it before adjusting again.

Be sure to check the reach when buying a new bike – you don't want to be too cramped or too stretched reaching for the handlebars.

Tips for elite time triallists

Once you have the general set-up right, it may be time to get someone to have a look at you to make sure you haven't become complacent in your riding position – you may, for instance, have become more supple over the last couple of years and have the ability to adopt a flatter, more efficient, position.

For time trialling it's all about riding fast and this can only be achieved by making yourself as aerodynamic as possible. Getting low is the best way of penetrating the air and this usually involves lowering the handlebars so the tribars don't prop your shoulders up in the air. You may need to fit a short, inverted Ahead stem or look at using a frame that's smaller than you'd normally choose, so you can get low at the front end.

Get your forearms in line with the bike so they are 'aero'. Check the width of your bottom bracket so that your feet are as close together as possible – this will make your own personal 'envelope' as small as you physically can. This is often referred to as 'the frontal area'.

Check the height of your saddle and its position over the bottom bracket. A tall, upright saddle position will present the maximum amount of your leg to the breeze, which is going to create lots of drag. Relaxing your saddle position to the rear and lowering it to around 109 per cent of your inseam will ensure that you get maximum power from a more relaxed position, making you more comfortable over the longer events. Working on trunk suppleness and strength definitely helps with this one!

If you're naturally bandy then it may be best to adopt a wider arm position so your arms precede your legs in the same airflow, rather than both occupying their own space and creating separate drag. Conversely, if you can get your elbows and knees together, your narrower overall profile will create less drag with the airflow tending to go around, rather than through, you.

2 Commuting/touring bike position

When you're touring you need to be comfortable. There's no point in setting out on a one- or two-week tour if your riding position is going to cause you grief and ruin what should be an enjoyable time. If you take the road bike position and shorten the reach by 5cm (2in) you won't go far wrong. You can also add the same amount onto the height of the handlebars so that your back is unstressed and you can spend time on the hoods or drops without having to regret not taking time to get the position sorted before you leave home.

The gears and brakes need to be freely accessible so that you have immediate control of your bike, which is likely to be laden with heavy panniers. Similarly, the handlebars need to offer plenty of choice for hand positions as you search for variety during the hours in the saddle. It's also a good idea to double up on your handlebar tape or use a more padded tape to cushion your hands on the trail.

Touring bikes tend to have a more laid-back seat angle than racers so you can expect to feel more relaxed, especially when grinding up hills. This is particularly important, as getting out of the saddle may be difficult when the bike is loaded. The head tube will also be more relaxed so you automatically reduce the reach to the handlebars without resorting to ultra-short handlebar stems.

Overall, you should be able to look up at the trees and the sky without craning your neck. The balance between saddle and handlebars should be correct so you don't have too much weight on your wrists. This way you should feel as though you can ride until the sun goes down...

3 Time trial bike

You can drop a frame size or two when using tribars, as it's your elbows that rest on the handlebars, rather than your hands. Reducing the reach to the handlebars is crucial so that you can crouch over the bike in relative comfort. Quite how low you get depends on your suppleness and confidence in racing on the roads in a prone position, where breathing and ultimate control may be compromised to some degree.

Aim to get your back or chest relatively flat so that the air passes by you without being scooped up, causing extra drag. Your mid to upper forearms need to rest on the tribar pads as opposed to your wrists which won't support you skeletally, causing early fatigue. You may need to find a pair of tribars that have rear-positioned pads so you can find good support without having to crawl all over the front of the bike. Don't just bang a pair of tribars onto your road bike and expect to get away with it. Doing this would undoubtedly over-stretch you and put you in a position of poor control. Fitting a shorter, lower stem usually adapts your road bike position into time trial mode but you may struggle to get low enough if your existing head tube is too tall.

Putting your upper body prone may cause a lot of discomfort if you don't tilt your saddle nose down a little. Consider moving it forward to put you in a more aggressive, power-position over the pedal bracket. If you do move your saddle forward, lift it out of the frame so that it moves in an arc rather than horizontally, which would push you down closer to the pedals.

2

3

Buying a new bike

People start riding bikes for all sorts of reasons, but what keeps them riding is that cycling is so addictive: once it has you in its grip you'll be looking for any excuse to nip out for a quick pedal.

The easiest way to ensure that you want to ride your bike is to get the right bike in the first place, one designed for the type of riding you will be doing, and one that fits you. These days there are many different types of bike on offer, at every price point, so choosing the right one can be quite daunting.

First you need to think about what kind of cycling you are going to be doing and then decide on what kind of bike you need – see pages 26–29 for which bike will suit your lifestyle.

Next set a budget – make it realistic, though, something you can afford and stick to. Don't forget to allow for any accessories you may want: clothing, gloves, a helmet or maybe some extras such as mudguards, a rack or a bag. You will certainly want a lock and lights.

Whatever type of bike you are after always try to buy the strongest, lightest one you can afford. These days, thanks to advances in materials and design, strength is pretty much a given. It's worth paying as much as you can to get a lighter bike simply because you are the bike's engine: less weight equals less effort required to get going, sharper acceleration, and being able to ride longer distances.

How much to pay?

A new bike needn't cost a fortune – you can get good mountain bikes for under £200. Good city bikes come in at around £250, and expect to pay around £300 for a budget road bike. If you want to race either on- or off-road, entry level bikes start at around £600. Budget folders can be had for £150, while well-regarded touring bikes can be had for under £500. You can also purchase mail-order or supermarket bikes for under £100, but they are likely to be heavy, with inferior brakes and gears, and they may well be poorly put together too. Look at it this way, a cheap bike that you ride once is money down the drain – an expensive bike you ride all the time is an investment.

Be prepared

Before hitting the shops it is worth doing some research – this will not only save you time but it could save you money, too. Check out the bike magazines for reviews of likely bikes, dealer listings and dealer advertisements. Most bike manufacturers have websites with information, and also a list of dealers – some of these, particularly the big national and regional chains of bike shops, also have websites – making it easy for you to compare prices. Not all manufacturer sites will give prices, and those that do usually post suggested retail prices – a few clicks to dealer websites or calls to the shops themselves will often reveal deviations from this price, usually in your favour.

Don't limit yourself to looking at just one bike to start with, have options. A little time spent on research will give you a feel for what's out there, at what price, and give you a wider choice to pick from. Have at least a couple of alternatives lined up so you've got something to compare your first choice to.

At the shops...

When you get to the shops have a good look at all the bikes you are considering, then ask to test ride a couple of them. A lot of shops are a bit cagey about this, but if they want your money they should be prepared to let you have a go; you might have to leave a credit card or some security behind though. If you can get a test ride make it a good one, a bike can seem ideal if you just take it for a spin round a car park, but to be sure, you really need to test it over a few kilometres/miles, and try to ride a hill or two. Don't try one bike – test your alternative choices as well to get some comparisons. The shop may not have a demo bike in your size, but make sure that they have the real thing to fit. It may be that you fall between sizes – as a rule it's better to go a bit smaller than a bit bigger, a bike that's too big may be harder to control. A good shop will adjust a smaller bike's set-up to suit you by fitting a longer stem. If you're prone to impulse buying, leave your credit cards at home. That way you won't be seduced, and it will give you a bit of time to assess your needs.

Doing the deal

You've done your research and you've been for the test ride, now it's time to get that bike. Ringing around the bike shops and checking websites should have given you an idea of the range of prices for your chosen model. You may simply want to go for the best price but if that involves having to travel, take this into account. On the other hand there may be a shop nearby who can't quite match the price but may be prepared to do a deal. They might not discount the bike but many bike shops will often be willing to make up the difference by offering you parts and accessories such as mudguards or a lock. Going after the best deal is fine, but remember there isn't much point in putting noses out of joint for the sake of a few pounds – particularly if it's your local shop and you are going to want to go back for spares or advice, and to get your bike serviced. The shop that will give you the best deal in the longer term may not be the one selling the cheapest bike.

Pound stretchers

If your budget doesn't quite stretch to the bike of your dreams, don't despair. It may take a little extra time, leg work or both but there are ways of maximizing your outlay, as long as you don't mind getting last year's model. Bikes do change annually but often it's a matter of paintwork or minor 'evolutionary' changes.

Most manufacturers change their ranges every year. The big mountain bike firms – who also make road bikes – usually change over in September; road firms traditionally change over at year end. So in September 2006 most 2006 bikes will become 'last year's' model and, depending on what they have left, shops will start discounting unsold bikes. September is therefore a good time for bargain hunting, as is February when it's cold, grey and most people are broke – if you've got money to spend you'll get a very warm welcome at your local bike shop.

Buying a second-hand bike

Buying a second-hand bike is a good way of getting a lot for your money.

There are bargains to be had, but remember it's a case of buyer beware. If you don't know much about bikes take someone who does along with you when you are looking to buy one. Try to get as much history as possible, and original receipts if available. Take a torch or bike light with you to help you see inaccessible bits of the bike. Know your frame size (see page 30–35) and take a tape measure with you to check the size of the bike.

Remember that a bike is only a bargain if you are going to use it. Make sure it fits you properly and is the right bike for your needs.

When looking at a bike that needs work ask yourself, can I do the repairs myself? What will the parts cost? If you can't do it and need the services of a professional, what will parts and labour cost? Then ask yourself if the bike is still worth buying.

What to look out for

- Components that are covered in grime as this is a sure sign the bike hasn't been looked after. If the seatpost is rusty, you won't be able to adjust it.
- A bike that has been in a crash could be unsafe, so check the forks (the top third of standard raked forks should be in a line with the head tube) and look for signs of welding or kinks/ bulges in the paintwork, especially in the area where the down tube joins the head tube. If you can, check that the wheels are not buckled.

- Check that the bottom bracket cups are tight by rocking the pedals – if the cups can be seen to move the bottom bracket shell may have become ovalized, which is costly to repair.
- Lift the bike and spin the wheels to check they're true and that the bearings turn smoothly – if in doubt take the wheels out of the frame to feel the bearings.
- Take a ride on the bike to check for smooth gear shifts and sound brakes.

What if your bike doesn't fit you?

Don't be put off riding it, as there are ways of fixing the problem...

It can't be stressed enough that having the right size bike is the best way to ensure an enjoyable riding experience, but irresistible second-hand bargains or hand-me-downs may result in you riding a bike that's too big or too small for you.

If you want a road bike for training and longer day rides then a frame that's too small can be adapted. You might well turn it into a time trial machine as a shorter reach to the handlebars and a lower handlebar height are exactly what you want when using tribars.

However, if you really want to persevere with a small frame for the road you can replace the standard handlebar stem with a longer, more upswept version to create more reach and height. The seatpost may need replacing with a longer equivalent to get your leg length right. Be aware that smaller frames generally have steeper seat angles (to falsely create a shorter top tube) so you may want to push the saddle back in its rails for a more relaxed pedalling style. A small frame may well come with narrower handlebars so measure them up and be prepared to replace them with something that's as wide as your shoulder joint width.

If the frame is too big it's possible to fit a shorter handlebar stem to reduce the reach. If the handlebars are still too high you could get rid of the existing stem and use an A-head converter, which would enable you to fit a short, inverted mountain bike A-head stem.

If you can achieve your correct leg length then riding a large frame should be fine as long as there's enough standover clearance to give you confidence for rapid dismounting, etc. If the handlebar position or standover clearance is not to your liking after making the necessary modifications then it really is best to either sell the frame or the complete bike and start again.

Things to check

The seats and handlebars of most bikes can be adjusted in a number of ways to suit the rider or type of riding, and help avoid pain or injury. Check regularly that the following is correctly positioned for you: the seat height, the seat position, the saddle – this should be level, or tilted forward very slightly for greater comfort – and the reach, angle and height of the handlebars.

Buying at auction

Do you wince at the prices of shiny new bikes? Or just want a hack?

Why not try a police cycle auction? They are an excellent way of picking up a bargain as retrieved stolen bikes whose owners fail to claim them are auctioned off to the public. You could find anything from bikes with customized, top-quality componentry, to pink and blue kids' bikes with stabilizers, to ex-hire bikes still with their identifying tags.

These auctions take place all over the country throughout the year. To find your nearest police cycle auction, ask at your local police station.

Another option is to check to see if your local auction house offers a bicycle sale. Often these are a chance

for second-hand dealers to purchase stock but they can be just as useful for the individual buyer. Some, like Lloyds International in South London, even auction unclaimed stolen bicycles on behalf of the police.

Auction tips

Go with a set budget – and stick to it. It is easy to get caught up in the event – especially if the auctioneer is a good one!

Find out how the auction works before you take part. You have to register to bid and you may need to pay a cash deposit to take part, though this is fully refundable if you don't buy anything.

Remember when you buy things at an auction, you have to pay the auctioneer's fee (usually 10 per cent) in addition to the price the hammer fell at. Some items are also subject to VAT in addition to the lot price and the auctioneer's fee.

Note that bikes sold at auction are sold as seen. Descriptions are to distinguish between lots, there is no guarantee they are correct, so examine the one you are considering closely.

Remember that auction goods have no warranties and are not covered by consumer legislation.

If you're not sure what to look for in a second hand bike it might be a sensible option to take someone else along with you. Ideally this should be someone who knows a bit about bikes, but they could also simply provide moral support and make sure you don't get too carried away in the auction atmosphere!

Cambridge bike auction

Ten past nine on a Saturday morning and it's the police cycle auction in Cambridge. The bikes are stacked against each other: you can't move them to examine them. There are Dutch bikes, good-quality mountain bikes, catalogue bikes, kids' bikes.

The crowd is surprisingly varied – as is to be expected in this city, which has two universities and several colleges, there are a lot of students. There are also couples and collectors. Anyone who is here to buy has registered as they walked in and received a card with a number.

People congregate at the back of the room where a table has been set up close to the back door. At 10 a.m., the first bike is brought through and is given a once over and the findings relayed to the auctioneer and the crowd: 'Ladies' blue bicycle, large frame, working brakes, broken back mudguard'; 'Gents' specialized red and silver mountain bike, rideaway condition...'

The auctioneer opens the bidding. For the first hour or so you might pay anything between £40 and £80 for a good bike. Hang around until the end, when most of the students have left pushing, riding or carrying their (they hope) bargain buy, and with fewer people to bid, the prices aren't pushed up so far. If it's bits you are after, you might get 'unreadable remains' free if the organizer can't face carrying it back to the store.

An average of 100 bikes go on sale at each Cambridge auction, increasing to 250 in October. Police spokesperson Nicky Phillipson says the bikes come from 'all over the place'. There are two main sources. Either the bikes are: 'found and handed in and not claimed' or 'seized' from thieves. Nicky explains that when the police recover a bike they check it against the descriptions of stolen bikes. Details of the good-quality bikes are put onto their website. Nicky says too often people reporting their bike as stolen can't provide a sufficiently detailed description (make, model and frame number) to enable police to check bikes they do recover against. Too many simply say, 'Er, it's a blue bike.'

About 3,500 bikes are lost or stolen in the city each year, of which 1,500 are recovered and returned to their owners. But, she says, some are bikes students leave behind or dump and some are 'fit for nothing'. Under the Police Property Act, bikes are liable for auction after 42 days in police custody. Profits from the Cambridge auctions go to a local charity.

Bikes are sold as seen, says Nicky. She advises that potentially dangerous bikes are not excluded from going into the auction, 'as some people buy them for the parts'. She says, 'The onus is on the [new] owner to get the bike checked over and to make it roadworthy.'

But is it legally yours? And what happens if someone claims to recognize the bike you bought at auction as theirs that was stolen? 'Though, technically, you could be taken to a small claims court, once you have got a receipt from an official auctioneer, it's your property,' says Nicky.

Assembling and checking your bike

If you buy a bike by mail order it's going to need home assembly and a check over. This should take just one or two hours, and is fairly straightforward as long as you have 4, 5 and 6mm Allen keys.

Most mail order suppliers are now very thorough about preparing a bike before sending it out – but it should still be carefully checked over and some assembly will be required such as fitting the pedals (often not supplied) and fitting the front wheel.

1 Initial assembly

Remove the seatpin bolt and smear anti-seize grease on its threads before refitting. Smear some anti-seize grease on the seatpin too and fit with the saddle to the frame – initially just insert the minimum amount of seatpin into the frame. With a straight edge check that the saddle is set exactly level – if not, adjust it by loosening the seatpin bolt on the pin – even with best micro-adjust seatpins you may need to make a couple of attempts before it is exactly correct. Align the handlebar stem with the frame and tighten its fastening bolts.

2 Pedals

Check that you are fitting the correct pedal to the crank. Most are marked with either a L or G for left or R or D for right. Smear some anti-seize grease over the threads before refitting to the cranks. Screw the first few threads in by hand in the same direction that the crank turns when pedalling. For the right-hand (chainwheel side) pedal turn the pedal spindle clockwise and the left-hand pedal spindle anti-clockwise.

3 Measuring your bike

Measure your current position before setting up your new bike. Measure saddle height from platform of pedal to top of saddle with the crank lined up with seat tube. Measure saddle set back – the distance between the nose of the saddle and a vertical line that bisects the bottom bracket spindle. Use a plumb line to find where the vertical line falls and measure from there to the saddle nose. Measure the handlebar reach from the rear of the saddle to the handlebars. Measure handlebar height – the difference in height between the top of the saddle and the tops of the bars.

5 Positioning the front derailleur

Check that the height of the derailleur is such that the cage clears the top of the large chainring's teeth by 1–2mm and that a centre line through the cage runs parallel to the chainrings. If adjustments are necessary, slacken the derailleur fastening bolt by about two turns so you can easily move the derailleur up and down and side to side. After adjustments refasten the derailleur mounting bolt and check that it is still positioned correctly. Finally shift the front derailleur onto the small chainring and check that the cable has no slack. If necessary, slacken the cable fastening bolt.

4 Setting the bike to the right dimensions

Adjust the saddle height. Measure the saddle set back as above, loosen the saddle mounting bolt and slide the saddle forward or back to the correct position. Recheck and readjust the saddle height if you have moved the saddle. Now check the saddle to handlebar distance. If this is incorrect by more than 1cm (2^1/$_2$in) you will need to buy (or exchange your old stem for) a new one which will achieve the correct reach. Check the difference in height between your saddle and the handlebars.

6 Front derailleur shifting checks

Shift onto the largest rear sprocket. Check that the chain shifts without hesitation without overshooting the small chainwheel inwards. If necessary adjust the low gear limit screw half a turn at a time either to make the shifting cleaner (anti-clockwise) or to prevent overshifting (clockwise). Shift into the smallest rear cog. Repeatedly shift to the biggest chainring – adjusting the high limit screw half a turn at a time until it does so without hesitation, without overshooting the largest ring.

7 Rear derailleur stop adjustments

Shift into the smallest sprocket. Visually check that the upper derailleur cage pulley is in line beneath the smallest rear sprocket. If not, adjust the limit screw until the pulley is exactly in line with the sprocket. Shift into the lowest gear (largest rear sprocket). Visually check that the upper derailleur cage is in line beneath the largest rear sprocket. If not, adjust the limit screw until the pulley is exactly in line with the sprocket. Carefully check that the chain cannot overshift the largest rear sprocket.

8B Campagnolo rear cable adjustments

To adjust the indexing, shift onto fourth smallest sprocket and adjust the cable tension adjuster so that the pulley is positioned beneath the fourth cog. Turning the cable adjuster anti-clockwise moves it inboard; turning clockwise moves it outboard. Shift to the fifth smallest sprocket. Turn the adjuster a quarter of a turn anti-clockwise if the change is slow or hesitant, or if the top pulley is not perfectly lined up with the sprocket. Check the shift in the reverse direction. If it is slow, turn the adjuster back (clockwise) an eighth of a turn.

8A Shimano rear cable adjustments

Select top gear and turning the pedals forward, select the next gear. If the chain doesn't move smoothly to the next sprocket turn the adjuster clockwise half a turn at a time until the chain moves cleanly to the next largest sprocket. Select the next largest sprocket and check that the chain will move cleanly to it. If not, turn the cable adjuster clockwise a further quarter of a turn at a time until the change is clean. Check that the upward shifts are still okay. If not, back off the cable adjuster (turning anti-clockwise) until the shifts are correct.

9 Brakes

Check that the brake blocks are mounted firmly and that they do not rub the tyre. Check that the brake to frame fixing nuts are tight. Check that the brake lever mounting bolts are properly tightened and that the levers are level and straight on the handlebars. A long straight edge across the top of the lever hoods will help you see whether the levers are level with each other.

10 Headset and tyres

Check that the forks rotate freely and without play –
if not, adjust the headset. Loosen the stem/steerer
clamp bolts. Loosen the top cap bolt off and then
retighten until all play is removed from the headset
whilst ensuring that the forks still rotate easily. Take
care to get this adjustment exactly correct. Align the
stem with the forks and tighten the bolts that clamp
it to the steerer. Pump your tyres up to the correct
pressure and you should be ready to ride.

Top tips

- Many frames get a paint chip during assembly.
  Be especially careful when tightening any
  bolts close to the frame that nothing slips.
- For derailleurs with limit screws on the rear
  face (Shimano), the high gear limit screw is
  the upper one. With limit screws on the front
  face of the parallelogram (Campagnolo), this
  is normally the lower one.

Essential accessories **2**

Helmets

Choosing a helmet is first and foremost a safety choice – you are buying head protection.

All other considerations are according to taste, head shape, budget and needs. Which is not to mean that they don't matter – fit, build quality and retention are not just about comfort, looks and convenience, but safety too. The very minimum standard you should insist on is the European voluntary safety standard CE EN 1078. But, given that testing standards around the world emphasize different aspects of a helmet's safety, the more regions it is certified in (especially the stringent American Snell, Canadian and Australian/New Zealand standards) the safer it is likely to be. Unfortunately, lack of the relevant sticker doesn't necessarily mean that a particular helmet doesn't conform to a particular country's standard, as 'stickering cost' may have meant they've been left off. Almost all the other buying criteria, such as colour scheme, fixing systems and price, will always be subjective and dependent on each buyer's specific head shape, taste, wallet and needs. As ever, try extensively before you buy...

A helmet with winter accessories. The kit includes insulated ear flaps and vent plugs to block the air flow, keeping your head warm. See page 140

The fit

A correctly fitted cycle helmet should sit level on the head, not tilted back or forward. It should be snug enough that without the strap fastened, it does not move about, but not so tight as to be uncomfortable. It should be impossible to roll it off your head with the straps fastened. Try a variety of different makers' helmets and pick the one that comes closest to your head shape. Make sure that you spend time getting the right fit. There's no point buying the safest helmet available if it won't stay on your head.

There are so many makes and models of helmets, you will need to shop around before you buy to ensure you make the right decision and find the best fit for you. See page 140

How helmets work

Cycle helmets are designed to protect your head when you fall off your bike onto the road, or dirt. They are NOT designed to protect your head if you hit something hard like a wall or car. Most people will agree, however, that in the event of hitting something hard like this with your head, it's better to have something to cushion the impact. Brain injury and damage occurs when the head incurs sudden deceleration and a good helmet will slow this down to an acceptable level. Some helmets absorb the impact of a fall by deforming and breaking in some instances, although many modern helmets are designed to stay together, hence the importance of a decent bonded over-shell, for secondary impacts. The outer shell should be smooth to discourage any friction when skidding (down the road) and, also along these lines, the outer profile should be rounded to avoid neck injuries caused by snagging. Peaks, visors and mirrors could all present a catch hazard so need to detach easily in a fall.

When to buy a new helmet

Helmets should certainly be replaced after a good knock but, apart from that, a helmet should last several years. If you have any doubts, destroy your helmet to prevent putting anyone else at risk. And if you have broken strap buckles then replace them immediately, or buy a new helmet!

Does more money equal a better helmet?

It seems that in safety terms it isn't the case that a higher price equals a better helmet, but that more cash actually buys enhancements, such as extra vents/lighter weight that serve no real purpose for a lot of non-performance cyclists. If you are after a basic helmet then take time to look through the stickers inside the helmet.

Women's helmets

Do women have different shaped heads than men or is the female-specific helmet just a marketing ploy for women to spend more money? It depends on the size of your head – average to large heads won't find anything wrong with a standard helmet and will have the best choice of lids and prices. Small heads will have problems, especially in the low to mid price ranges. Head sizes below 54cm (21in) will find that unisize helmet shells don't work, and no matter how much padding you add, the fit won't be secure or safe enough to endure a big crash. Anyone with a smaller head will need more adjustability on the straps, both across the chin and to the rear (the retention system cannot be expected to take up all the slack), so make sure the shell fits pretty well first.

Care of your helmet

Treat your helmet with the utmost care. Transport it with your hand luggage, rather than with your bike and wash it in warm soapy water only. Most helmets have removable pads so you can wash these individually and put them somewhere to dry. Do not subject helmets to high temperatures.

Helmet safety ratings

There are a number of safety standards, the main ones to look out for are: ASTM, CPSC, TUV and Snell. In America, all bicycle helmets must meet the CPSC standard. **ANSI (American National Scientific Institute)** ceased to function in 1995 and should now be ignored.

ASTM F1447 (The American Society for Testing and Materials) The ASTM is one of the world's largest voluntary standards development systems with more than 10,000 standards published annually. Rates alongside Snell B84 for toughness but uses a rubberized head form during tests, which lowers effective safety rating. Now moribund due to CPSC. See www.astm.org

Australian and New Zealand standard 2063: 1996 – Pedal Cycle Helmets If you wear Met, it may well pass this standard. In some respects it's more stringent than CPSC – see the Bicycle Helmet Safety Institute at www.bhsi.org for a comparison of World standards.

BSI (British Standards Institute) Specification for Pedal Cyclists Helmets BS 6863:1989 was withdrawn and superseded by the English Language version **EN 1078**, in 1997, prepared by the Technical Committee PH/6. EN 1078 is a slightly less effective standard compared to the old BS 6863 it replaced but way behind Snell B90/95 or even the earlier Snell B94.

CE (European Committee for Standardisation)/EN Products with CEN certification carry a CE marking. This does not indicate conformity to a standard, but to the legal requirements of European Union directives. The mark is not a certification of quality, either, but indicates that the manufacturer claims compliance with the directives that apply to the product. The CEN develops voluntary European Standards, such as the EN 1078 found alongside the lonely-looking 'CE' on your helmet sticker.

1080 CEN European Standard Impact Protection Helmets for Young Children Almost the same as bicycle helmet standard EN 1078 but the buckle has to release at a force of 9 to 16 N to help prevent hanging accidents on playground apparatus or when climbing trees. Don't let your kids play off the bike while still wearing their helmet...

CPSC (Consumer Product Safety Commission's standard) All helmets manufactured in America after March 10, 1999 to be applied must by law meet the CPSC. The first standard to be applied in a uniform and mandatory way, the CPSC can be found on Giro, Specialized, and Bell - who used CPSC to oust the tougher Snell. See www.cpsc.gov.

ISO 9002 A 'quality', not a performance, standard achieved by some manufacturers. It means that the particular company is working to established procedures at all levels in order to prevent mistakes and/or improve existing products and services.

Snell Inspectors can swoop on a shop to test samples, and have the power to recall helmets countrywide if they fail. Snell standards concentrate on impact absorption, positional stability, strap strength and the area of the head protected by the helmet. Snell B90 is comparable to ASTM and CPSC but Snell's newer B-95 standard is the most stringent in the market – more difficult to meet than the ASTM or CPSC standards. Snell has been effectively squeezed out of bicycle helmets due to market forces. The best motorcycle helmets in the World use Snell. www.smf.org.

TUV/GS A qualified product safety testing and quality certification organisation that can certificate to CE/EN 1078. The Personal Protective Equipment (PPE) Directive, 89/686/EWG, defines the basic safety requirements that PPE must meet. PPE makers who want to gain a marketing advantage can pursue GS Mark or Q-Mark certification to show that their products have met superior safety and quality characteristics. www.uk.tuv.com.

Lights

There is a legal requirement for lights to be fitted and used on a bicycle during the hours of darkness, but it is really just common sense for you to make sure that you are visible to other motorists, pedestrians and cyclists.

Even though as a cyclist you can often see without using bike lights as your route is lit by streetlights, it does not mean that someone can see you. So put on your lights as soon as the sun starts to go down or if visibility is seriously reduced.

When it's dark you need to see and be seen, which are two different things. There are not many lights that can accomplish both tasks, but mix your lighting up a little and you can have such a set-up, and you won't be breaking the bank to achieve it, either. At the front, you want a light that other people can see, not only from directly in front of you, but also from an angle, such as when approaching road junctions. If you add to that a light that gives off a good direct beam to light your way (when the streetlights run out, or that towpath/Sustrans route gets too dark) then you are well on your way to having an effective lighting set-up. Add a good rear light, and preferably a rear reflector as well and you're almost set to go. A reflective strip or two on your jacket or some kind of reflective accessory added to your clothing or bag won't go amiss either. Getting a good, simple low light riding set-up isn't rocket science, but it could spell the difference between meeting a car at high speed, or having it stop because the driver has seen you.

There are lots of different lights to choose from, ranging from budget battery models for short-distance urban commutes through to rechargeable and dynamo options to powerful off-road rigs costing well into three figures. Your minimum requirements should be a front light with a distinct beam and a bright red rear light.

Battery filament bulb lights

These lights with a single bulb are the mainstay of b i k e lighting, as they are reasonably cheap to purchase and easy to use. They use ordinary batteries, which will typically last for only about six to eight hours, although some will last for longer. They are therefore best used for infrequent dusk and night-time riding.

Reflective vests

Available from all good bike shops, supermarkets, iron mongers, etc., the traditional reflective vest or tabard is not to be scoffed at. They offer excellent visibility from a very long range in the path of vehicle headlights, they're cheap, easy to put on, and save more lives each year than any other device for riding a bike at night.

Another similar option is a reflective band, which will again make you more visible to other road users – look for one that is waterproof and adaptable.

Rechargeable battery lights

You only tend to be able to buy rechargeable front lights, but often they will come with a separate LED rear light. The extra cost of buying rechargeable lights is soon recouped by the fact that you don't have to buy batteries for the lights. Best used for commuting and longer night-time rides.

Front and rear lamps (above and left) are essential for riding and will often come as a set. See page 140

LED (Light Emitting Diode) lights

LED lights operate for hours on a single set of batteries, which makes them very useful if you are a regular night-time cyclist as they make you very visible. At present it is illegal to use flashing LED lights, although this law will soon be changed. You can, however, use non-flashing LED lights as long as they conform to Standard BS 6102/3.

Dynamos

Lights that don't need batteries have never worked better. With continued improvements to battery-powered lights, why would a commuter, in particular, choose a dynamo system (above)? Well, unlike the former, they are always ready and unlikely to get stolen, lost, fall off, forgotten or run out of juice. They will cost less to run as they don't need batteries, and can even weigh less than a comparable battery set-up and its possible spares too. They will, however, cost more to purchase initially, so if you are only using them rarely it may not be worth the extra money.

Few high-power battery lights use a cycling specific focused beam, so a 3 watt dynamo lamp can compete well for illumination of the road, and often provide a better side visibility 'halo'. Dynamo units are, however, pretty useless off-road because most only reach full brightness at speeds of about 9–13km/h (6–8mph). Older dynamos will also need you to pedal in order for the light to work; some newer dynamos work for a while even if you are stationary.

There are two main types of dynamo: tyre-driven and hub.

Tyre-driven or 'bottle' dynamos

Tyre-driven dynamos rest against the side of the tyre and are driven via a rotating wheel. They have the

obvious advantage over hub dynamos of zero drag when not in use, but for commuters this is not an issue. They also weigh less and generally cost less, too, making them better for occasional use. But, on the other hand, in adverse conditions, such as mud, snow, ice, and rain for poor-quality models, it is possible for the pulley to slip, giving you no light at all just when you need it most.

Careful setting up is required to ensure reliability and avoid excessive wear of the tyre sidewall, but once set up properly, bottle dynamos rarely cause problems.

Bottle dynamos run best on tyres with a dynamo track, which could limit your choice. Some trial and error may be required to find a good, non-slip, low noise combination. Traditional mounting brackets can damage the paintwork and even the frame, so use a brazed-on mounting if possible. Never use a clamp-on bracket on the forks because it can slip down the blade and go into the wheel.

Most models come in left- and right-sided versions: a left model fits to the left side of the fork blade or seat stay, facing backwards.

Hub dynamos

The great advantage of hub dynamos is that they are very efficient, are silent, cannot slip or wear the tyre, and are virtually 'plug and play' units with nothing to set up or adjust. They are, however, heavier than bottle dynamos (by about 200g (7oz)) plus are more expensive as you will need to get the hub built into a wheel, which will involve new spokes and labour costs. So don't forget to lock your precious wheel!

Locks

As long as there are bicycles in the world there will be people who want to steal them – any bike left unattended is a potential target.

In the UK alone about £32 million worth of bikes get stolen every year. Of course, there is a simple mechanism for reducing the number of thieves out there – the bike lock. If every cyclist carried a lock and used it properly bike theft would be an awful lot harder, and there would be an awful lot fewer bike thieves. Bike thieves don't care what type of bike you ride – whatever it is, if you let them, they'll nick it. So do your bit to cut crime by using a lock, and using it properly, particularly when you are on the move and likely to be leaving your bike unattended for some time, as that is when your bike is at its most vulnerable. Remember that it only takes a few seconds for a thief to take an unlocked bike.

Security

These days there are plenty of different locks available for all situations: U-locks, cables, chains for on the move or at home, nurse's locks and even nifty little immobilizers for those café stops where you are away from your bike but you can still see it. Plus there are static security devices for at home or work (see page 92) as it's a sad fact that theft from sheds, homes and workplaces is an ever-present threat too.

As ever, lock manufacturers can't afford to stand still in the fight against crime – bike theft may be a numbers game and mainly an opportunist crime, but that doesn't mean to say theft techniques aren't evolving all the time. In Britain the favoured method is still brute force, but the growth in ever more powerful portable power tools is adding extra firepower to the thieves' arsenal. In response a number of locks have been made noticeably harder in recent times. The balance manufacturers have to strike is that if they harden their locks too much they risk making them brittle.

In the past some manufacturers have made a lot of the pick-proof nature of their locks, partly because in other markets this is a favoured technique. Up until now we, along with all the police forces we have spoken to, have dismissed this as irrelevant in Britain, but recently the City of London Bike Squad has reported a rise in these sorts of thefts. However, lock picking is still very much a minority pastime – and despite what you may hear about wonder tools being available over the internet, it is also an art requiring patience and practice. Those who perfect it tend to move quickly on to higher value goods – once they are old enough to drive...

Which lock?

Which lock or locks you need depends on where you will be leaving your bike. If you have a very secure area in which you can leave your bike at home and at work then you won't need a heavy duty lock; but if you are leaving your bike at the station every day then you probably want to invest in a good D-lock and possibly a cable too.

There are three main types of bike lock: cable locks and chain locks; shackle locks (D-locks and U-locks); and immobilizers.

Cable locks

Cable locks are popular as they are very portable, light, flexible and reasonably priced. The thicker the cable, the harder it is to cut, but also the heavier and less flexible it will be. Portable cables are therefore often easy to cut through – it's expecting a lot of a cheap cable to think it will withstand a power tool for any length of time. Don't rely on a cable lock as your sole security device, although they do provide a visual deterrent, which is better than none at all. A cable lock is therefore best used as a secondary device in conjunction with a decent U-lock or chain as you can secure the more nickable bit of your bike's componentry such as the saddle, bottle cages, etc.

Security advice

Whatever type of lock you use it pays to follow some simple rules:

- Always lock your bike. A lock is no good in your bag.
- Fill as much of the shackle or cable with as much bike as possible as any slack can be exploited.
- Always make the lock mechanism itself as inaccessible as possible; if it's hard for you to get at it's hard for the thief too.
- Lock your bike up in plain sight and never lock it to something easier to cut through than your lock, such as a tree or fence.
- Never lock your bike up somewhere quiet and out of the way where a thief can really take his time. The maximum most thieves will spend trying to nick a bike is five minutes, unless you make it easy for them.
- If you commute have a really solid lock (and chain) where you regularly park your bike along with something lighter and more portable in case you want to stop en-route. Or, you could fit an immobilizer to the bike.
- Don't leave commuting locks on railings or bike stands to which thieves might have access – it gives them the chance to practise on your lock.
- Never leave your bike unsecured for even the shortest time. You might as well put a 'Steal Me' sign on it. Always make the thief work.
- A bad lock is better than no lock and a poor lock well used is at least equal to a good lock badly used.

A cable lock (left) serves more as a visual deterrent than a real security measure. If you have no second lock, such as a shackle lock (opposite), use a well known brand name to deter thieves. See page 140

Chain locks

Chain locks are stronger than cables – the strength is determined by the type of steel it is made from and the space between the links. However, they are heavier and therefore less portable than cables.

Shackle locks

Shackle locks are made of hardened steel and comprise the mechanism housing and a U-shaped round bar, the ends of which fasten into the mechanism. They are excellent because they allow you to securely lock most of the important parts of your bike and are one of the most secure types of locks that you can purchase. However, they do have their limitations – they are heavy so aren't easy to transport, and aren't large enough to secure all the parts of your bike, so a D-lock or a U-lock plus a good cable is even better.

Immobilizers

Although not a high-security device, a lightweight immobilizer is ideal for café stops as it's small and very transportable. Breaking it would be simple, but for quick stops where your bike is in sight it's a handy gizmo. Bike theft is nearly always an opportunist crime, so never leave your bike without locking it.

It may also be worth investing in a frame-fitted immobilizer (or loop lock), which loops around the wheels to prevent the bike from being ridden away. It is common in Europe and is favoured by numerous British police bike squads for their own steeds.

Cheap locks

A cheap lock is better than no lock. So, do you get what you pay for? The answer of course is that there's an awful lot of margin in a lock – mainly for the shops. Most come out of China with a unit price in pence. Most of us wouldn't expect much from a cheap lock but bump up the price and, well, it might be okay... At least most of the expensive locks work and their manufacturers can part justify the cost in terms of covering their R&D budgets and building their brands. And bike thieves are brand conscious too. An Abus or Kryptonite logo can be as much of a deterrent as the actual lock.

What to buy

There are three things to bear in mind when buying portable security devices: first, you get what you pay for. Cheap locks offer cheap security: most are little more than a visual deterrent, which is not to say no deterrent (a cheap lock is better than no lock) but should a dedicated bike thief take an interest in your bike, say goodbye to it.

Second, cable locks that are light enough to be portable are also light enough to be broken – easily. Only use them in conjunction with a good U-lock to secure extra bits of the bike or stuff like your helmet.

Three, less is NOT more. Unlike most other bike accessories the performance of a cycle security device increases in proportion to its weight. So when it comes to portable locks it's a trade-off between how much peace of mind you want and how much metal you are prepared to lug around.

Sold Secure

Many manufacturers have their own security ratings and these can be a useful indicator of the expected level of performance. Even better, though, is a Sold Secure rating. Most of the major lock makers now submit their products for testing by Sold Secure: an independent non-profit-making organization, which was originally set up by Essex and Northumbrian Police with the backing of the Home Office, and is now administered by the Master Locksmiths Association which test the locks and certify them. There are three levels of Sold Secure rating: Gold, Silver and Bronze, which denote the length of time a lock will hold out against escalating levels of attack. A Bronze rating indicates that a lock will hold out for one minute of attack using basic tools; a Silver rating denotes three minutes against more sophisticated weapons; and a Gold rating shows that the lock will last five minutes against a full tool list as used by the dedicated/professional thief. Gold rated locks can be more expensive but it is worth noting that some cycle insurers will insist on a Sold Secure Gold rated lock as a condition of their cycle insurance.

The largest manufacturers also have their locks accredited in other countries – the German and Dutch standards are both particularly worth looking for.

The Bic issue

When Chris Brennan posted a Quicktime movie of him opening his Kryptonite lock with a Bic pen on to a US forum, all hell was let loose as US cyclists replicated his feat on their own locks using Bics or similar. The Bic flick and numerous imitators spread around the US in days and the resulting product replacement program will cost Kryptonite millions. The fact is, though, that this method does not work on all cylinder locks, we're talking old locks, and cheap locks. As far as we can tell it was one particular type of cylinder that was affected and its use was certainly not limited to Kryptonite, Masterlock were forced into a product recall too, and there are plenty of other brands out there that were using the same cylinder. Finally, it doesn't appear that the Bic method has ever been favoured by bike thieves as brute force is still the average thief's chosen way.

The controversy about cylinder locks and Bic pens, which proved big enough for even the mainstream media to take notice, has probably hastened the exit of cylinder locks, but they were on the way out anyway.

What else to look for

Warranty: an extended warranty is always good. It's not going to cover you against theft but it should be a sign that the lock won't fall apart or seize up on you.

Anti-theft guarantee: basically a form of insurance pioneered by Kryptonite. These inevitably bump up the price, but they definitely add peace of mind to the package.

Will it fit? There's no point buying a shackle lock that is too small to go around your bike. On the other hand, too big means you are going to have difficulty filling the shackle, and it's going to be awkward to carry around. A longer shackle should be easier to twist, easier still if it isn't filled.

Mudguards

Getting rained on is bad enough, but the constant spray of cold, dirty water from your wheels on a wet road – even after it has stopped raining – is worse.

Unless you ride in full cycling kit and are happy to soak it, you'll want mudguards.

You can fit some sort of mudguard to any bike. They might not make the bike look any cooler, and they will make it a bit heavier and less aerodynamic, but the payoff in keeping yourself and your bike drier and cleaner is well worth it.

Here we're primarily looking at mudguards that will fit road bikes and sports hybrids – bikes where the clearance for mudguards is an issue. If you've got a touring bike or urban mountain bike with loads of clearance and the right braze-ons, just fit whichever of the SKS P-series of mudguards best suits your tyre size. They're still the benchmark mudguards for road use, and they come in sizes to suit 700x20c road tyres (P35) through to 26x2.3in mountain bike slicks (P65).

Nuts and bolts

Full-length mudguards often don't come with the Allen bolts (or fork crown bolt) that you need to fit them to the frame. Don't leave the shop without some. When fitting, make sure the Allen bolt on the drive side mudguard eyelet isn't so long that it touches the chain on the smallest sprocket.

Stays

Four stays per guard (two each side) are more secure and stable than two, although a few bespoke mudguards have a single pair of much heavier gauge stays, which work fine. If you use a rack, mount the mudguard stays outboard of the rack stays.

Safety

If anything gets jammed under the front mudguard, it can stop the bike dead. The mudguard can fold up behind the fork and jam. For this reason, some mudguards have stays that are designed to pop out of their plastic end pieces when force is applied. This safety feature is highly recommended.

Coverage

Partial mudguards provide partial protection. They'll keep the worst off. Full mudguards stop spray better, but won't always keep your shoes or a following rider from being spattered. Mudflaps are the answer. Buy dedicated ones or make your own (e.g. from an ice cream tub lid, or other stiff, pliable rubber).

Tyre clearance

The more space there is between tyre and mudguard, the less likely anything will jam there. A gap of 10mm ($^1/_3$ in) or more is recommended; less than 5mm ($^1/_6$ in) is asking for trouble. Fit the front guard as high as possible under the fork crown (bending the top of the mudguard bracket if it interferes with the headset race), and fit the bracket behind the fork. If the guard won't fit safely under the fork crown or seatstay bridge, don't make it: instead, cut it short and bolt it on behind.

Brake clearance

With V-brakes and full-length mudguards, check that the 'noodle' is able to clear the guard. If it's lower than the bottom of the fork crown or seatstay bridge, then even with a long bracket, it might not be high enough. Sidepull brakes are rarely closer to the tyre than the part of the frame they're attached to, but they can foul the side of the mudguards if these are wide or have deep sides. Cantilever brakes are usually fine with any mudguards.

Toe clearance

A front mudguard eats into the space between toe and tyre. It's rarely a problem on mountain bikes and tourers, but on road bikes and sports hybrids it may create or exacerbate toe overlap. If your foot hits the mudguard, it'll interfere with steering and you may end up taking a fall. While it's generally only a problem during slow speed manoeuvres, it's still something you need to be aware of.

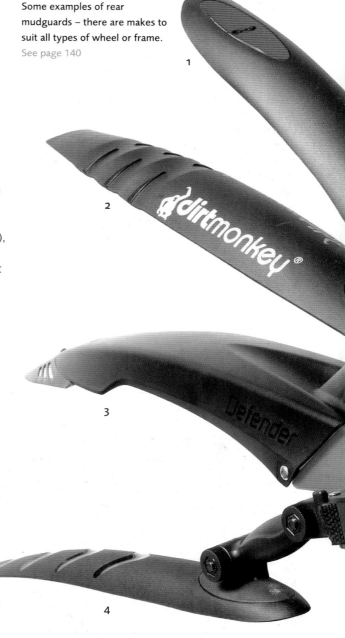

Some examples of rear mudguards – there are makes to suit all types of wheel or frame.
See page 140

1

2

3

4

Other accessories

Don't forget these essential extras...

Pump

Tyres need air so get a pump (right, and below). Unless you've got a lot of bikes a mini or frame fitting pump is all you need. These, as the name suggests, are small, highly portable devices that you can either carry around in a bag or mount on the frame. The more sophisticated are suitable for both high volume tyres (as found on mountain bikes) and high pressure tyres (as on road bikes); some have fitting mechanisms that automatically adjust for either Presta or Schrader valve types. There are even pumps containing CO_2 cartridges which take the effort out of inflation entirely.

EXPECT TO PAY: £3–£30 for a mini pump.

Tools

You may not be into home maintenance, but even so you will have to tighten the odd nut and occasionally adjust your saddle, so at the very least get a set of Allen keys and a box spanner. If you want to be even more prepared get yourself a multiitool, there are loads of cycle specific ones available containing all the relevant Allen keys, plus screwdrivers, chainsplitters and lots more besides.

EXPECT TO PAY: £2–£5 for a set of Allen keys; £10–£35 for a multi-tool.

Puncture repair kit

Further essentials are a spare inner tube (below) and a puncture repair kit (left). Don't waste time trying to mend a puncture by the side of the road. Instead, get the tyre off, check it for whatever caused the puncture, then replace the punctured tube with your spare, inflate it and you are on your way. You can repair the punctured one once you get back to the comfort and convenience of home.

EXPECT TO PAY: A puncture repair kit plus tyre levers should set you back about £3, a spare inner tube £4.

Bell

Last (but definitely not least) a bell, ideal for warning pedestrians you are there, especially when riding on cycle paths. If buying new, your bike should be fitted with one already as a legal requirement.

EXPECT TO PAY: About £5.

You may not need some of these items immediately after you buy them, but they will become indispensable in the long term. See page 140

Child seats, trailers and helmets

Cycling is a great way for children to explore their surroundings and get out in the fresh air, whether as a passenger or, when older, on their own bikes.

Child seats

Child seats are the traditional answer to the problem of transporting small children by bicycle. They're not as visible, as stable, as protective, or as capacious as child trailers, but they're not as expensive either. They also require less leg- and lung-power, so for some journeys, especially in better weather, they are a good option.

You can purchase either front or rear child seats. Children are ready for a child seat when they can sit up for long periods; usually by the age of about nine months. Four or five years is the normal upper age limit for a seat. The main restriction is weight: the safe load limit of the seat and the load that you can safely cycle with behind you is usually between 18 and 22kg (3–3 1/2 stone).

Fit the child seat to a bike with wide flat or riser handlebars to give you maximum control and leverage. Make sure you've got a triple chainset, unless you're very fit or live somewhere flat. And fit the fattest rear tyre you can get away with: more airspace equals more comfort for your passenger.

Handling

Even a small child can add the equivalent of a couple of loaded panniers to your bike, so handling can be severely compromised. Panniers put the weight around or between the axles while rear child seats put the weight above and – more importantly – behind the rear axle. Get a plumbline and aim to ensure that the base of the seat back is no more than about 10cm (4in) behind the rear axle.

Before you take your child out for a ride in the seat, load it up with a heavy weight – a 10kg (22lb) sack of spuds would be ideal – and take that for a spin to accustom yourself to the bike's compromised handling. You can stabilize the unbalancing effect to some degree by using low-rider panniers up front. Front child seats don't have such a dramatic effect on handling (although they force you to ride bow-leggedly!), but it's still worth taking the aforementioned spin with the potatoes. Also, make sure you practise getting your leg over the top tube without swinging it over the saddle, or you'll kick your passenger in the head!

Safety

Safety is paramount with any child-carrying device – and what price your child's health? Today's wrap-around style moulded plastic seats offer some protection if the bike falls on its side, and they mean that feet in spokes are a thing of the past. Beware anything else going in spokes, like mittens-on-strings. And if you have a sprung seat, be sure to zip-tie on a home-made plastic guard to prevent small fingers finding their way in between the springs...

Look for a waist belt or grab bar, in addition to the three-point over-the-shoulder harness. Children can slump at any angle when asleep and you don't want them to dangle dangerously over the side of the seat. In fact, that's another reason for getting a seat that reclines or that in some way supports a sleeping child.

Extras

Consider fitting a twin-leg centre stand as it can be difficult getting a child into and out of a child seat if you're on your own.

If you find it hard to balance when looking round with your passenger on board, fit a mirror – not only will you be able to monitor traffic behind you, you'll be able to see if your child has fallen asleep.

If you have a seatpost fitting rear light, a child seat will obscure it. Fit a light to the back of the rear rack instead.

Helmets are essential for child passengers and cycling children (see page 65).

What to check for

- Ensure that the age/weight range is suitable.
- How secure and safe is it?
- Does it recline, and if so, how easy is it to do so? With young children this is especially important as they tend to bob forwards.
- How easy is it to fix the child seat to the bike?
- Check handling/stability, especially on bumpy ground.

Front-fitting and back-fitting child seats: a great way of taking your kids with you. See page 140

Child trailers

Trailers are becoming more and more popular, and most trailers will carry one large or two smaller children. Most suit children from four months to nine years – the recommended minimum age is actually nine months (the sitting up stage), but you can secure an infant's car seat in a trailer using luggage straps. Harnesses are provided so that children are strapped in securely and safely, and windows are incorporated into the trailer so children can see out.

As the drag of a loaded trailer is noticeable on even the slightest hill, the towing bike needs a low bottom gear (under 25in). Good brakes are equally important when descending, but shouldn't be used suddenly or the trailer may disconcertingly shunt the towing bike.

If you're a trailer bike heavy-user or plan to ride longer distances, it may be worth investing in a trailer that fixes to a rear rack and articulates on ball bearings. These are more stable and less tiring for you, and they follow the towing bike's back wheel more faithfully.

Trailer bikes may look bulky, but storage shouldn't be a problem as most fold flat. All the top brands come with a range of accessories and many also convert into stroller/joggers.

Advantages of a trailer over a child seat

- Much greater capacity (two children, plus room for nappies, toys, groceries etc.).
- Better bike handling.
- Protection from weather (sun, rain, wind) and insects.
- Trailers are safer than seats. They're more visible and wider, which encourages drivers to give you room. If you fall, the trailer should remain upright; even if it doesn't, the children are protected by a roll-cage.

Trailer bike

A trailer bike is essentially the rear part of a normal child's bike, which is attached to the seat pillar of an adult bike, so that an older child (four to nine years) can be towed. The child can pedal as much or as little as they like independently of the adult, and some better models even have brakes and gears for the child.

Child helmet

Fit is the most important criteria for a helmet, so rather than looking for a specific model, visit your local bike shop and choose one that sits snugly on your child's head. It should be British Standard approved. Make sure it's worn properly, with the forehead protected rather than exposed. Avoid over-tight straps or nipping your child's neck with the clasp by sliding a finger behind the chin-strap when fastening it. Ventilation isn't very important – passengers don't generate much heat.

If buying a helmet for your child, then put the helmet on them yourselves, as they might not be at ease with the shop staff. Choose a helmet that fits safely on the day of purchase, but has room for growth between the inner harness and outer shell.

Note: Do NOT let your child climb trees or play on apparatus with their helmet on. Despite it seeming a good idea, children have been hanged by their helmet straps following a fall.

Top tips

- Fit a crudguard to the down tube of the trailer bike, up near the handlebars. Your passenger's face is in the line of spray from your back wheel.
- Use mudguards on the towing bike, if possible, and get two racks or hitches so you can swap the trailer bike between towing bikes.
- If you'll be riding at night, you must fit a rear light and reflector to the trailer bike as it will obscure those of the towing bike.

Racks and panniers

Using racks and panniers really opens up the world of bike travel – whether it's the daily commute, a weekend in the countryside, or a few months on the open road.

Keeping loads off the shoulders, racks and panniers literally take the backache out of both touring and riding to work – once tried, you'll appreciate what an advantage they hold over your rucksack for any ride longer than a few kilometres/miles.

In fact, panniers have come a long way since their humble origins – delivering freshly baked baguettes down cobbled French backstreets. Nowadays they're available in a huge range of materials to suit every pocket and intention – with roll tops, bolt-on pockets, ingenious release systems and even funky designs. Outwardly simple, panniers are constantly being improved.

There are new ideas filtering into the rack realm too, as riders look to extend their horizons, both on and off-road. After all, fitting the right carrier to hang your bags on is just as important as how you carry your kit. The meanest, toughest touring machine is one thing – but if your rack can't match its cargo, it will shimmy like a rattlesnake slithering across the road. Likewise if you're commuting, there's no need to burden yourself with heavy-duty steelwork designed for the Serengeti.

Trailers are another option. Add to this a range of bar bags, saddlebags and rackpacks, and before you know it your faithful steed will have taken on the size, shape and load-hauling duties of a Bactrian camel.

Rack materials

The best racks are generally made either from aerospacegrade aluminium rods or tubular steel. Which one you need depends on what you're carrying, where you are going and how far you are travelling. Light and stiff, aluminium racks are amply sufficient for moderate loads on good roads – Blackburn set the ball rolling in the 1970s and is still the benchmark. Steel's advantage is that it's less prone to fatigue and it's generally repairable – just pop in to your friendly local welder. The best steel racks are as light and stiff as their alloy counterparts. If you intend to pack in the weight, make sure your rack is heavy duty enough not to flex under serious loads or you will find that your bike's handling is compromised.

Pannier materials

Pannier bags are largely split into three categories: welded, nylon (Cordura) and Cotton Duck.

One hundred per cent waterproof panniers use high frequencies to weld seams together. Based on early designs of truck tarpaulin sewn together, the process was pioneered by Mr Ortlieb in the early 1980s and it's a testament to his foresight that most companies have now adopted their own versions. Encased in PVC (tougher but eco-unfriendly) and Cordura (lighter), different weights of material are available with different resistance to abrasion – if holes do wear through, you'll need to patch them up with a special kit. Welded panniers tend to be simpler in design with fewer pockets.

Cordura or other nylon panniers are more traditional and can be advantageous in having extra pockets and zips for easy access to kit and snacks. Though they can be water repellent, the seams will let in moisture. Most nowadays include a waterproof, high-vis shell, stowed in its own pocket. Although not absolutely effective, it should keep out all but the very worst storms – though you do have to stop to put it on, restricting access to the bags.

Lastly, Cotton Duck is a super hard-wearing, easy to repair material tried and tested over years of expedition touring. It's both breathable – so damp clothes won't go musty – and its fibres expand in the rain to keep moisture out. In practice, Cotton Duck is 95 per cent waterproof – on really prolonged downpours bagging any valuables is a must.

Watch out

Keep an eye on your racks when touring, particularly on bumpy roads. Even tiny repetitive movements wear divots in the tubing, so wrap contact points with electrical tape, both to protect the finish and reduce play. Check bolts every few days, or apply a few drops of Loctite to prevent them working loose – stainless steel bolts are less prone to snapping than aluminium. Ensuring that bolts are long enough to run completely into the mounting eye also helps.

P-clips are fiddly to set up but are useful if you don't have eyelets on your frame – they should be available at your local DIY store. Wrap the stay in electrical tape to reduce the chance of it slipping and gouging your frame. If you don't have any dropout eyelets, Tubus now produce axle-mounted fittings. Even better though are Old Man Mountain racks that use a skewer through the hub and V brakes as fixing points. If you're running disc brakes, callipers sometimes interrupt the rack leg – particularly with cable pull versions. While the rack can sometimes be spaced out with an aluminium rod, Tubus's fixings for disc brakes are designed to work with their own models by moving them further back.

When fitting panniers, make sure there's enough room for heel clearance. Aim to keep loads located as directly as possible over the rear axle and keep the mounting clips spaced wide to stop the pannier bending out at the sides. Even the toughest panniers can get damaged from day to day, so try not to lean your loaded bike carelessly against walls, to reduce abrasion. Your pannier first-aid kit should contain a strong thread (or dental floss) and a thick needle for repairs. Welded seam panniers are harder to fix effectively so it's wise to carry a spare set of patches and glue with you, and then apply patches to both inside and outside.

Panniers are a wonderfully simple and efficient way of carrying around extra material. Some fit to the front wheel of your bicycle as well as the rack. See page 140

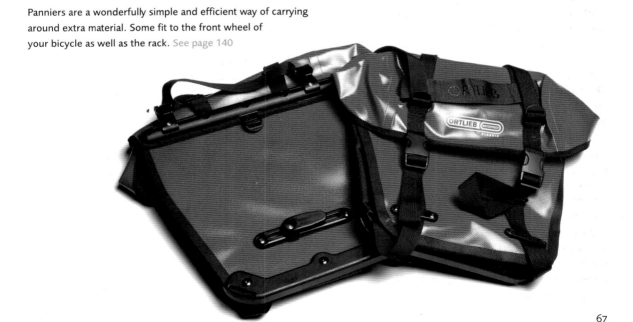

Other styles of load carrying

While the humble rucksack is probably the easiest option for quick and lightly loaded rides, particularly on your mountain bike, it's best to try to keep weight off your back when you're touring or on longer commutes.

Bar bags: Up to around $8\frac{1}{2}$ litres in capacity, bags which hang on your handlebars provide the perfect, easy to access space to store a camera, valuables, sunglasses, snacks and the like; the only downside is that weight at the handlebars compromises handling. Heavily loaded, they'll also cause your handlebars to swing round, so make sure there's enough give in the cable routing. The best are waterproof, easily detachable and feature a map case. Padded inserts are available for some, but if you're running suspension forks, keep the load as light as possible.

Rackpacks: Up to 15 litres in capacity, rackpacks are better suited to fast riding. They're more aerodynamic and keep weight away from the handlebars, while providing enough space for lunch, spares and a waterproof top. Though well-padded, vibrations make them less suited to carrying cameras.

Saddlebags: Up to 24 litres in capacity, saddlebags are very much a British institution. A handy alternative to two small panniers, they hang below the saddle and would be best suited to a larger frame.

Front racks

Unless you're keeping to warm climes, camping tours may require four panniers, especially on a tandem. Low riders, which sit at hub level around the front wheel, help distribute weight, improve handling and plant the front wheel on steep climbs. Front racks above the wheel offer better clearance off-road but aren't as stable. If you want to tour with suspension forks, remember they're not designed for loads, so keep weight minimal.

Off the bike

Many panniers come with a removable strap to supplement handles – useful for lugging up a long flight of stairs. But for off-the-bike exploring, panniers are notoriously awkward to carry. A lightweight and foldable backpack is handy for day trips and, over an extended walk, is better for your back than a bar bag.

Security

While most panniers can't be locked, you'll find people quite amenable to keeping an eye on your bike – cafés are a good option, especially if you're giving them some business. Bar bags are handy, and pocketless panniers offer less temptation – you can always stash your dirty underwear on top as a deterrent!

Parking

When laden bikes fall, they fall hard, so it's generally safest to lean them against something. Tie a loop of thin cord round the handlebar grip to squeeze the brake shut and stop your bike rolling forwards or backwards.

Propstands are particularly useful when there's not a tree in sight. They also avoid scuffing your panniers – the trouble is they're not designed for fully laden bikes, so they tend to snap in time. Most are braced against the seat and chain stays at the dropout end.

Packing your kit

While two panniers and a bar bag should be ample for hostelling and warm weather tours, you'll probably need four for longer journeys, particularly if you're camping. It's better than trying to cram everything onto the rear rack; minimalists might even get away with just a couple of front panniers on the back.

Try to keep weights even on both sides of the bike. How you split the weight will depend to a large extent on your bike. Conventional packing wisdom advises a 60/40 ratio on the back/front. Some frames prefer considerably less up front, while others are better suited to an even load. Shift the weight around until you get the most predictable, shimmy-free handling.

Everyone hones down their own preferred packing system after a few days on tour, though you should try to keep heavy items, such as tools and spares, as low as possible to improve handling. Dividing kit by type – kitchen, tent, clothes, etc. – keeps things easy to find. Mesh bags are an easy way of making sense of clothes, particularly if your panniers lack compartments – or try mesh laundry bags as a cheap alternative. However tidy you are, a couple of bungees are always useful for strapping on paraphernalia – try motorbike shops for a good range. Roll bags increase your capacity, and some are designed to clip onto your panniers.

If you're using a stove with a fuel bottle, stash it away from pots and pans or you'll be tasting pasta à la petrol all holiday.

Bike racks for cars

For when you want to take your cycling further afield.

Only those with people carriers or camper vans will have enough space to carry their bikes inside their vehicle when going away for a weekend or longer. Travelling by train with a bike is increasingly difficult too, so attaching your bikes to the exterior of your car is important for touring or racing.

Which system is best for you?

There are plenty of types of rack to choose from. Each type has its advantages and disadvantages. You need to think carefully about how you're going to use your rack and your car before deciding on the type

Pros and cons

The three main types of rack available all have their benefits and drawbacks.

Strap-on racks

Pros: Relatively inexpensive; you don't need special fittings such as towballs or roof bars. Easy to fit.
Cons: Easy to fit badly; less secure; scuffed paintwork.

Towbar mounted racks

Pros: Secure; easy to fit; bikes/rack won't damage paintwork; easy to lift bikes on and off; you can use boot.
Cons: You need a towball; they can be pricey; your car needs an electric hook-up; you may have to buy a light unit; extra length can make parking tricky.

Roof-mounted racks

Pros: Bikes are up out of the way; you can open your boot easily; they don't make the car any wider; if you've got roof bars the world is yours.
Cons: You need roof bars; they aren't cheap; you have to lift bikes on to the roof; increased drag; mind that bridge/car park entrance!

to buy. With roof and towbar/towball mount racks it is essential to consider the weight of the rack and your bikes. Your car manufacturer will have a maximum recommended weight for the roof bars and a maximum recommended noseweight for the towbar: neither should be exceeded. With towbars and roofs it is typically around 50kg (110lbs). Although hatchback doors and boots don't have a weight limit, we don't recommend carrying more than three bikes this way and preferably only two. Hatches, doors and boots are not designed to carry loads.

Strap-mounted racks

Strap-mounted racks are simple racks that rest against the back of the vehicle and are attached by a strap. They need care in fitting in order to be really secure. They cannot be used on fibre-glass hatchback doors, and all glass rear doors will need special fittings. Strap-mounted racks are best used just for fairly short trips, as straps easily work loose over longer journeys. Most use two arms to support the bikes – and these are not kind to your bikes. With normal low mount car racks a lighting/number plate board will be essential, so while these are the cheapest racks available you'll need to budget for the cost of having a lighting socket fitted, and the price of a lighting board. High mount racks get around this problem by putting the bikes higher up, but they cause a lot more extra drag (thus increasing fuel consumption) and create higher stresses on the rack, the bikes and the car's hatch or boot.

Towbar and towball mounted racks

Towbar mounted racks will carry two, three or four bikes and are ideal if you already have a towbar (add extra to the cost if you don't). The most common type features two arms to hold the bikes, just like the strap-mounted racks, and are either fitted to a plate behind the towball or on the towball itself. Some models allow you to tow at the same time. The other type of towbar rack carries the bicycles by supporting the wheels, which puts less strain on the bikes.

Towball racks that mount the bikes low down on the back of the car cause less wind resistance, thus reducing fuel consumption compared to putting the

bikes on the roof or on a highmount back rack, and they also tend to put less strain on the bikes and require less lifting. They're also very secure and don't require much skill to fit them – though they are typically a more expensive solution than the alternatives. You'll need a towball for a start, and low racks will also often obscure the number plate and lights – so a lighting board together with electrics will be a necessity too.

Roof-mounted racks

These fit to standard roof bars. Most cars can carry two bikes and some up to four this way. You need to buy a rack for each bike and cost in a set of bars. Most hold the bike via a support arm and clamp that fastens to the bicycle's down tube and with straps holding the wheels to a trough. Generally they're secure and the bike is easily lockable. The pro teams normally use racks that clamp the forks and with a strap to secure the rear wheel in a trough – these are normally very secure, quick and easy to use. But the roof bars must be positioned according to your bike's wheelbase ±10–20cm (25–50in), which is not possible on some cars with built-in rack mounting points.

Top tips

- Do not obscure the rear lights or the number plate with either the rack or the bike. It's an offence, and you can now be fined on the spot for it.
- Depending on the rack, protect your paintwork with a regular household cleaning cloth. Don't use something so soft it makes the grip between bike and rack slippery – that's the best way to lose your bike.
- Although so-called aero bike covers exist for roof-mounted bikes, the increase in frontal area is so great, they actually increase drag, increase fuel consumption and increase the strain on all mounting points.
- Lock your bikes together and if possible also lock them to the rack. It only takes a few seconds for a deft thief to remove them from a rack.
- For hook-on racks that wrap over the edge of a boot or a hatchback, to make sure they are not going to wreck your paintwork, get some helicopter tape (the clear protective tape that is self-healing) and apply it to the car, not the inside of the rack. It's soft enough to offer plenty of grip for a well-installed rack, but tough enough to protect the paintwork from accidental damage.
- If you have a towbar system stick a post-it note on your bike the night before you leave. On it write 'electrics'. When you put your bike on the rack you'll see it, and remember to plug in the electrics, or at least rip it off safe in the knowledge you already have.

Strap-mounted racks are the least expensive and don't require any modifications to your car – but watch out for your paintwork!

Clothing for cyclists

There are no hard and fast rules. You can choose to have as much or as little cycling kit as you want.

Performance rider

Race kit isn't just for racers - if you do any type of performance cycling this is the sort of stuff to look at. There is plenty of kit crossover from the leisure market (the jacket pictured) that is equally useful for hard riding. If you ride hard and fast, your kit must be able to deal with heat and sweat, and be durable.

Even in winter, most fast riders won't need more than a light wind and shower proof jacket that fits in the back pocket of a race jersey. Shorts tend to be lighter weight for the road, slightly heavier for off-road – and there are plenty of styles on offer: shorts for summer, longs for winter, three quarters – a good all year round choice – and all are also available as all-in-one bib shorts, bib longs, etc.

Leisure/commuting

If you are going on longer weekend rides, or you feel the need for speed on the ride to work, then technical clothing makes sense. As well as gloves, you may want to protect other vulnerable parts by wearing cycling shorts. You've got two choices here: figure hugging Lycra or baggies which look very much like a normal pair of shorts. Both Lycra shorts and baggies will have a padded insert usually made of some sort of synthetic chamois. Lycra shorts come in four, six, eight or even ten panel versions: the more panels, the more they move with you and the more comfortable they should be. More panels cost more money too, of course. Look for flat stitching and an insert that suits your shape – men's and women's shorts have different shaped inserts.

Short distance commuter

The main advantage of most cycle specific clothing is that it is designed to deal with sweat. But if you are only going a short distance, such as from station to office, and you're not trying to break any speed records on the way, you really don't need any special clothing beyond a pair of gloves, maybe a helmet, and a pair of cycle clips. You don't even need the clips if you tuck your trouser leg into your sock. Whether you wear a helmet is a personal choice, but we would certainly recommend wearing gloves and in the unlikely event you come off it will be your hands you put out to save yourself – so it makes sense to give them some protection. The other piece of kit we would strongly recommend you buy is something reflective – being seen is very much being safe when it comes to riding in traffic.

Winter cycling kit

Cold, wind, rain... luckily these days there is plenty of technical clothing available to help you not just endure the winter weather but beat it altogether.

The key is getting the right type of kit to match the weather conditions you'll have to face and the type of riding you'll be doing. Even on warmer days the wind can cause a huge drop in temperature as it hits you, and biking tends to exaggerate this, so the more protection you have for winter riding the better.

Before you start looking for the right kit, here's a few fairly obvious things to bear in mind. For a start, performance riders and fast commuters are not, in the main, going to need to wear as many layers as leisure riders, tourers or longer distance commuters. The other thing you need to factor into your kit buying is your own physiology: do you run hot, or cold? One last piece of advice: if you're a performance rider, warm up properly before you start – especially important in winter, and whatever type of riding you do, don't dress for the first five minutes of your ride – otherwise you risk overheating early on, sweating loads and then if you are on a longer ride risk having that sweat get cold. Believe us, cold and sweaty is a lot worse than hot and sweaty. All this may sound complicated, but it isn't because modern cycling clothing is both so well suited to the task, and so adaptable.

Use the Internet, local papers and an outdoor thermometer to work out what will be the best riding gear for you on the day. A little extra can always be peeled off, but get too cold and you can spoil a ride.

Base layer

A base layer is essential for maintaining a good body temperature and for keeping your skin dry; a close-fitting layer next to the skin 'wicks' or transports moisture to the outside. On warmer days you can wear a base layer under a jacket without a jersey and still benefit. Fit is essential: you need contact with the torso and a lightweight man-made fabric such as polyester or polypropylene to move moisture and vapour quickly and that dries in super fast time too.

The base layer is the building block of any layering system. It has one of the toughest jobs of all the layers. It must wick moisture away from the skin as moisture from sweat is one of the key factors in us getting cold.

While sweat in the summer is a bonus because it cools the body temperature, come winter time it leaves us damp and ready to be frozen. But wearing a base layer isn't just a case of wicking the wet away, it must also control our body temperature – too hot and we sweat too much, too cold and we don't perform. The cut is also crucial – low back, plenty of length in the sleeves, no chills to sneak in.

Mid layer

The mid layer is the artillery of the layer system and the one with most variants. Essentially an insulating layer that must maintain the warmth and bring traditional jersey features such as pockets, low back and high throat-protecting collars. With the advent of lightweight windproof fabrics this layer often has to be able to function as both a mid and outer layer in milder climes, hence some blurring of terminology with some midlayers being called jackets and others jerseys, or even the same garment being in a manufacturer's jacket and jersey range. This can make it a difficult one to buy. Strong assessment of your riding environment and the intensity of your riding will help in selecting a good mid layer, but you will probably need a couple of different options to suit different types of weather.

Women's mid layer

A female-specific jersey should take into account the cut around the bust and waist and offer a comfortable fit to suit the type of riding you want to do. Technical features are essential if you plan on riding hard; good ventilation and wicking properties are must haves; and fast drying fabric will keep you warm and dry.

Jackets

The best approach to looking for a new outer layer or shell is to decide what features you need, and what features you'd like. Do you want it to be highly breathable? Do waterproofing capabilities really matter? How many pockets do you need? Does your washing machine wash as low as 30°C? Is a hood a good idea? Do you have exceptionally long or short

Keep warm with base layer, mid layer and jacket. With so many designs and fits, you're sure to find one right for you.

See page 140

arms? It really does pay to sit down and work out what you really need, and set yourself a budget before you start shopping around. We know brand loyalty plays a big part here, and if you've had a very good garment from a certain brand in the past you are very likely to go back to that make first. But look around at what else is available.

Women's jackets

A good fitting jacket can make or break a ride in heavy winter conditions – so again, as with mid layers, cut is important. As well as the obvious differences, women tend to have shorter torsos than men and the cut of your jacket should take this into account.

A windproof jacket will allow you to ride all year round – and the more breathable the fabric, the better the performance. Gore-Tex is the industry standard, but there are many other breathable fabrics that allow you to stay dry. As a rule, the more you are prepared to pay, the better jacket you'll get; that doesn't mean to say that the most expensive is always the best, but with a bigger price tag things like taped seams and storm proof zips become standard.

Longs or overtrousers

Hard riders might be happier cycling in Lycra tights in the rain and changing afterwards. For normal clothes commuting and steady touring, you'll want overtrousers. Cheap ones can make you so sweaty and uncomfortable that you'd often be better without them. It's crucial that your longs protect the vulnerable parts of your lower half – knees, kidneys and crotch must all be adequately insulated. The crotch and seated areas need plenty of breathability to avoid sweatiness, and will lead to chafing and inevitably saddle sores, which can easily last a season and beyond.

In colder conditions a good supporting Lycra-based material will help avoid injury and support muscles through the dark season. Overtrousers are great for long rides or commutes. This might sound daft, but first off decide whether you are going to wear them over your trousers; if you are, make sure you buy a pair baggy enough to fit. If you're not, and you want them as an extra layer to go over longs or even shorts, make sure they are not going to be too baggy. Either way, if you are doing any sort of distance or riding at pace pay more and get breathable ones. Lastly, pay attention to how the legs cinch at the bottom particularly if you

have shorter legs and there is likely to be any bagging which could snag on the chainrings – disconcerting, and annoying.

Gloves

Your hands are the first part of your body to feel it when cycling in the cold. Warm and windproof are the top priorities for traditional winters. Waterproofing is secondary because arguably it's never that cold on rainy days. And while damp hands can be unpleasant, cold hands hurt. Many gloves come with a fleece lining, and sometimes a layer of Thinsulate. If they don't, add glove liners. These add warmth and can easily be washed and dried separately if they get sweaty.

Rainproof gloves are useful. Look for long, snug cuffs to stop your wrists getting chilly, and cover the cuffs with your jacket sleeves to stop rain running down your arms into the gloves.

Three other worthwhile features are pads on the

Don't forget your extremities!

There is a whole host of really useful bits of kit that you can use to bolster your existing cycling gear in winter or as an add-on to further beef up any winter buys, including gilets, thermal underwear and ear muffs.

The long-haul commuters and the heavy duty winter-trainers may benefit from leg and arm warmers. These have the obvious benefits of working well with shorts and short sleeved jerseys and they can be easily adjusted. Arm warmers are a great way of extending your protection without the commitment of a jacket – they prevent wind chill from sapping the heat from the forearms and wrists and are an invaluable autumn to spring addition to the clothing drawer. If it gets too hot, simply roll them up and put them in your back pocket.

Remember also to make sure that you are very visible, especially on dark and murky winter evenings. Wear something brightly coloured or fluorescent during the day and something reflective at night, such as a jacket belt, straps or trouser clips.

palm, especially over the ulnar nerve area (the heel of the hand opposite the thumb); a soft thumb for nose wiping; and either light-coloured gloves or reflectives on the glove back for more visible and safer signalling.

Women's gloves
The lack of women specific winter gloves is stunning. Granted, some manufacturers make XS sizes, but often these aren't quite small enough or specifically designed for narrower women's hands. Thankfully there are a

couple of women specific winter gloves on offer and if you want an everyday three season pair of gloves there's plenty more to choose from.

Shoes
A very useful piece of kit is overshoes – cold feet can really make a ride miserable. There are loads to chose from: lightweight, heavyweight, waterproof, windproof, thermal. Go for something that suits the type of weather you are likely to be riding in.

There is clothing available to keep every part of you warm and dry on a frozen winter's day. See page 140

Summer cycling kit

Summer is the time to get out and ride.

This can be in an organized event – road race, time trial, a charity ride – while touring, or just for the sheer pleasure of riding. But the weather, as we all know, can be unpredictable, so what kit should you have to be able to cope with everything mother nature can throw at you and, just as importantly, help you make the most of your time in the saddle?

You don't need to spend a fortune on your cycling kit, but having the right shorts, top and jacket can make your ride an infinitely more enjoyable experience. You don't want to be too hot, or too cold, you certainly don't want your shorts to rub uncomfortably. Any of these could ruin what might otherwise be a perfect cycling day out. We would argue that you need cycling shorts, but you don't need to wear lycra. There are plenty of 'baggies' out there suitable for cycling – and for wearing off the bike. And while some prefer lycra shorts, others, even in summer, swear by bibshorts for their extra comfort. As for jerseys and jackets, well there are hundreds to choose from, and there's no need to spend a fortune to keep dry, warm and comfortable on your bike. While there has been a wealth of men's clothes on the market for some time, women's cycling gear is now catching up and is constantly improving to cater for the expanding market.

Summer jackets

Uninterrupted sunshine is a bonus, but balmy blue-sky days can start or end with rain, mist or suddenly chilly weather. A windproof gilet, ideally with arm warmers, will let you tackle most rides in comfort. Unless you're riding hard, however, a gilet will only stand up to light showers at best. For extra weather protection, especially for those generating less body heat, it helps to have a jacket in reserve.

Complete waterproofing isn't usually required in summer, when the boil-in-the-bag effect of such jackets, even breathable ones, can make you damper with your own sweat than you'd get from a bit of rain seeping in via the shoulder seams. A summer jacket should nevertheless keep out the wind, along with the worst of the rain, and also allow perspiration to escape freely. Lightweight and low bulk are important for a

jacket that you'll be carrying more often than wearing. If it packs small enough to fit in a pocket or seatpack, you'll always have it with you; the best jacket in the world is no use at home. Reflectives are likewise useful for everyone, as is a high collar – to keep draughts out – and a good cut. Roadies are likely to want a simple shell with good venting for hard riding, and a dropped tail to cope with road spray. Pockets will be less important if a cycling jersey or gilet will be worn beneath. Tourers and commuters may want pockets for storage, and will rate weatherproofing and comfort as high, or higher than, venting and light weight. Anyone intending to ride with a courier bag, rucksack or hydration pack should note the position of seams, vents and rear zips. Seams can be uncomfortable, zipped pockets can be inaccessible, and vents can end up being covered.

Cycling jerseys

You have to decide what you want from a jersey before you go out and spend money. If you're a racer looking for a new top then you might have brands that you really like, and want to stick with them. For the higher end of the market, performance is what it's all about, and this usually brings with it the trade-off between hi-tech materials and washability. Most performance materials are machine washable, but only at 30°C. It might be worth looking at your washing machine for a moment. Does it go as low as 30 degrees? If not you're hand washing in the sink days are not over. For the recreational rider a pro-level top is really not worth the expense, and some riders who do not push themselves that hard physically actually find race jerseys too cold, even on hotter summer days. So look for something with good venting, that is breathable, and go for a slightly looser fit to allow air to move around. It really is a case of horses for courses. Fabric, design and cut vary between manufacturers, so where possible try before you buy. And work out what pockets you need – these should be large enough to carry the essential spares and positioned for easy access whilst on the fly.

Women's vests

Not your grim shapeless bloke's kind of vests, but all new stylish shaped little numbers with built-in bra supports and pockets. Unless you want to expose some cleavage, opt for high fronted designs that don't cause embarrassment when riding. Some vests have better built-in bras than others. Depending on the support you need, thicker shoulder straps tend to give better bounce restriction and avoid digging in too. There's a huge range in lengths as well, from the short, barely more than a sports bra, to hip-hugging long versions.

Shorts

Lycra shorts offer maximum comfort for cycling, and for mile-eating or racing they're unbeatable. Yet off the bike, for men at least, they offer a level of dignity comparable to a ballet dancer's tights – and who would wear those in public? They don't have pockets, either.

Mountain bikers, tourers and commuters often choose different shorts – long 'baggies' are the fashion among mountain bikers. Loose is fine as the air flow will prevent clamminess, although some may be heavier or flappier than you'd like. For comfort, look for sensibly-placed non-raised seams or a padded insert: thick is good on the bike but can feel a bit uncomfortable off the bike. Compromise, or get shorts with a removable insert. Side and rear pockets are more accessible on the bike than front ones. A drawcord allows a precise fit and keeps up shorts freighted with loose change, keys, etc. A zipped fly facilitates pit stops.

Women's shorts

Good shorts should be well fitting and comfortable both off and, more importantly, on the bike, and the padded insert should mould to your body and not fold or bunch up when in contact with the saddle. A smooth contact area is essential and thicker padding is a better choice for novice riders who may not have quite toughened up in the saddle region yet. Performance riding will require grippers around the legs to hold them in place but casual shorts without grippers give a more flattering look. Women-specific shorts often have wider and softer elastic waistbands – these tend to be more comfortable whatever type of riding you plan on doing.

Women's shorts used to be fairly expensive but recently prices have been coming down thanks to increased demand.

Gloves

Gloves are essential if you are riding in any sort of weather, and they also give extra cushioning for your hands and protection in a fall.

Summer cycling gloves, rather than keeping you warm, are designed to support and protect your hands. The palms are usually padded which helps stop any numbness. And if you find that your riding position puts a lot of weight on your hands, look for gloves with gel padding for extra comfort. Wipe away sweat with towelling or other fabric which many manufacturers put on the back of riding gloves (or mitts, as they are also known).

Shoes

Trainers or everyday shoes are fine for most commuting trips, although specialized shoes that clip into the pedals are available for the more serious racer. Don't forget, though, that all the energy you expend when cycling is transmitted through your shoes, so if your soles are soft or your feet are moving around, you are wasting effort. Make sure that any laces are tucked in so they don't get caught up in the chain.

Sunglasses

Glasses will keep wind, dust, and other irritants like insects or spray out of your eyes. And if you wear dark glasses you won't have to squint in bright lights. Glasses with interchangeable lenses are useful for protecting your eyes in all conditions – or, get yourself one pair for bright weather and one for dull weather.

Keep it light and simple: whatever your reason for cycling, investing in summer gear can stop you getting too hot, sweaty or uncomfortable. See page 140

Looking after your bike 3

The anatomy of a bicycle

Your essential guide to getting to know your bike.

1 BRAKE LEVERS Pull these to stop.

2 STI/ERGO SHIFT LEVERS Road bike gear changers that are integrated with the brake levers.

3 HANDLEBARS Drops, for road bikes (as pictured) which give a choice of handholds, and flat bars which give a more upright position.

4 STEM Connects the handlebars to the fork.

5 HEADSET SPACERS Only on A-head style headsets (see 7).

6 HEADSET This separates the fork from the frame.

7 HEAD TUBE Short front tube usually with maker's badge on it.

8 TOP TUBE Connects the head tube to the seat tube – often called the cross bar.

9 WATER BOTTLE Fits in a bottle cage on the down tube.

10 SADDLE Wider more padded saddles are good for slower riding, longer thinner saddles are best for distance and speed.

11 SEAT COLLAR A round clamp at the top of the seat tube.

12 REAR BRAKE Along with front brake (see 27), there to stop you.

13 CASSETTE (Or rear cogs).

14 SPOKES Connect the wheel hubs to the wheel rims.

15 QUICK-RELEASE SKEWER Sprung loaded skewer with a handle at one end and a nut at the other.

16 REAR DERAILLEUR (Or rear mech) shifts the chain between the cogs on the rear cassette.

17 CHAIN STAYS Near horizontal tubes connecting the bottom bracket shell to the seat stays.

18 CHAIN Connects the gears of the front chainrings with the rear cassette.

19 CHAINRINGS The front gears; attached to the crank arm.

20 CRANK ARM Pedals at one end, chainrings at the other: available in different lengths to suit the length of your legs.

21 BOTTOM BRACKET Cartridge mounted axle that joins the cranks to the frame – your bike's drive unit.

22 PEDALS Can be either platform, toe clip and strap, or clipless.

23 DOWN TUBE The diagonally angled tube from the head tube to the bottom bracket.

24 TYRE There are two main sizes: 700c for road bikes and 26in for

mountain bikes. Fat tyres give a more comfortable ride, thinner is faster.

25 INNER TUBE VALVE Through which air is pumped into the inner tube/tyre.

26 FORK Holds the front wheel and connects to the handlebars via the headset and stem.

27 FRONT BRAKE Use front brake to slow you down first and back brake to stop.

28 FRONT DERAILLEUR (Or front mech), this lifts the chain and moves it between chainrings.

29 SEAT TUBE Tube in the centre of the frame into which the seat post fits.

30 SEAT POST The post to which the saddle attaches.

31 SEAT STAYS The diagonal tubes on the frame which link the seat tube.

Bike maintenance

Know your bike and be prepared to fix it any time, any place.

Basic tool kit (see also pages 60–61)
Bicycle pump
Spare inner tube
Puncture repair kit
A set of plastic tyre levers
Light oil and grease
Cleaning rags
A set of Allen keys
A flat head and a Phillips head screwdriver
A set of spanners
Plastic gloves to keep your hands clean

Daily
Check your brakes. This can be done by putting the
front brake on and pushing forwards. Do the same
for the back brakes. The bike shouldn't move, and
your brake levers should not touch the handlebars.
Use your judgement – the brakes should work
without having to press down too hard on the handles.
   It's a good idea to have a quick look at your lights to
check they are working and that they are still bright.

Weekly
Use a degreaser, detergent or a specialist chain-
cleaning product to clean and oil your chain. Ideally
you should clean each link, then the chain rings at the
front, the sprockets at the rear and the jockey wheels.
Don't forget to oil the chain and all exposed metal
parts. Be careful not to leave excess grease as this will
attract more dirt. A light oil is best.
   Check your tyres, as the harder they are the less
vulnerable you are to punctures. If necessary, pump
them up as hard as you can with a hand pump or up to
the recommended listed tyre pressure point if using a
track pump or car foot pump. Double-check they don't
have anything stuck in them!

Monthly
Check brakes, gears and tyres (see page 88).

Fixing Punctures
Punctures can be caused by a number of factors
including low tyre pressure, if the liner that protects the
inner tube from the end of the spokes is decayed, if the
brakes are rubbing against the tyre making slices, or if
the inner tube is bulging out.
WHAT YOU NEED: Puncture repair kit (see page 61)

1 Take the tyre off
First, if it's a rear wheel puncture, shift into the highest
gear (smallest cog) before you start – this will make it
easier to get the wheel back on afterwards. Next take
off the wheel. On most bikes this involves undoing the
quick release (using the lever), but it may mean
unscrewing a nut on each side with a spanner.
   Next release the brakes – V brakes being the most
common, this is done by pinching them together and
slotting the cable out. To take the wheel off pull the
derailleur and lift.
   Once the wheel is off turn the bike upside-down and
sort out the flat. If there is a retaining nut on the valve,
take that off then unhook one side of the tyre from
the wheel rim using either your fingers or a tyre lever
to push against the spokes. Don't pull the tyre off
completely, just pull out the punctured inner tube
from under it.

2 Find the cause
There is no point mending the inner tube if the cause
is still stuck in the tyre, so carefully feel inside the tyre
for anything poking through and remove it. Check the
tube, if you can't diagnose what's caused the puncture
and you can't even see the hole, pump it up until you
hear a hissing noise then mark it with a piece of chalk
from your puncture repair kit. If the hole is on the same
side as the valve, check for a spoke poking around or
through misaligned or damaged rim tape. If there are
two slits that are parallel then the tube has been
pinched between the rim and the tyre. Check the
tyre sidewalls aren't damaged or worn.

1

2

3

4

5

3 Mend the puncture

On the go it's simpler to replace a flat tube with a spare and repair the puncture later. But take your puncture kit anyway – you may have more than one flat. Roughen the area around the hole with a bit of sandpaper, then apply glue to an area slightly larger than your patch. Let the glue go tacky to the touch then peel off the patch's backing foil and firmly press it on. Leave the top cover on the patch for a couple of minutes for the glue to set.

4 Clean up

Once you're sure the patch is stuck you can peel off the top cover. Now you need to dust the area of excess glue with chalk in order to stop the tube sticking to the tyre. Roughen the chalk on the back of the kit and use the dust to cover the glued patch. Inflate the tube to make sure it is fixed – if it's still leaking there may be another puncture or the valve could be damaged. If there is still a problem immerse in water to find any further holes.

5 Put the tyre back on

Partially inflate the tube and insert it, valve first, under the tyre and on to the rim. Start at the valve end and hook the tyre beading back to the rim. Getting the last bit on can be tricky and using a tyre lever can cause pinch flats so grasp the beading and use a rolling motion to get it on to the rim. Pinch the sidewalls to centre the bead and to ensure the tube isn't trapped or twisted. Replace the valve nut and inflate to the correct pressure.

Pull the chain up, which should be on the first cog, and press it back on, re-screwing the bolts or fastening the lever. Make sure the wheel is straight and the mudguards are clear. One thing that you mustn't forget is to re-connect the brakes!

Brakes

It's worth checking your brakes regularly, to ensure that they are working correctly and the brake pads aren't too worn.

WHAT YOU NEED: A 4mm and 10mm spanner, a small and big crosshead, a screwdriver and a multi-tool, which has different sizes of Allen keys (see page 60).

1 If your brake pads are old and are very worn then you will need to replace them. To do this undo the brakes, take out the old brake pads and replace them with new ones. Make sure that they're lined up and are positioned about 3–5mm away from the rims. If they're not, twiddle the adjusters near the handlebars on the brake cables until they are.

2 If your brake pads aren't hitting the rim at the same time then you'll need to alter the tension. This is done by gradually unscrewing the lower bolts on the V brake, testing them as you go until they equalize.

Gears

If your bike is juddering and clicking or even if it just doesn't feel the same as it used to, it's worth trying the following steps.

To understand gears all you have to know is that there are two derailleurs that work via a cable and what happens at the gear shifter influences what happens at the gear end. One problem is that cables can stretch, so the system loses tension to drive the derailleur.

1 Start with the back wheel by dropping back to the gear that the bike is happy in. Follow the cable along to the derailleur barrel adjuster and turn it outwards a quarter to add tension. To test this out, pedal the bike and keep dropping down and up the gears listening for clicks and screwing the adjuster until the problem's gone.

2 Switch to the front wheel and again follow the derailleur cable until you reach the right adjuster. Now repeat exactly as above.

Tyre and tube information

Sizing: There are principally two main wheel and tyre sizes for adult bikes: 26in and 700c. 26in are mainly found on mountain bikes and their many offspring; 700c on most types of road bike.

700c wheels are slightly bigger than 26in but like 26in wheels they come in a variety of widths. As a very general rule, 700c wheels are about speed whereas 26in wheels are about comfort and strength. 700c wheels tend to be narrower than their 26in counterparts, and again the narrower wheels (whatever their size) tend to be about speed and can take higher pressures, while wider tyres are about comfort and take a higher volume of air. However, there are tyres in both sizes that seek to combine comfort and speed – often for touring or commuting.

Know your size: Most tyres will have their diameter and width written on the sidewall: 700x23 or 26x1.5. 700s are sized in metric, 26in wheels in imperial. Sounds like a recipe for confusion? It is, especially as one manufacturer's 26in may not be quite the same size as another's. So when buying a new tyre it is better to trust the five-digit ISO number on the sidewall, which looks like this for a 700x28c tyre: 28–622. The first two digits are (roughly) the tyre's width (in millimetres), while the last three are the diameter of the tyre at the bead (the inside edge of the tyre), also in millimetres. If the bead seat diameters match, then the tyre will fit the rim. Of the more common wheel sizes, 406 is the 20in BMX size, 559 is the 26in mountain bike standard, and 622 is 700c. It's important to get tyre and inner tube sizing right because if you don't the tyre isn't going to stay on the rim.

Upgrading your bike

Do you want to make your bike faster, lighter or more comfortable? Here are five ways in which you can upgrade your bike.

Tyres

Probably the easiest and most cost effective upgrade you can make. First, to keep your bike running at optimum efficiency, keep your tyres pumped up to the correct pressure – soft tyres don't roll as well, so you have to pedal harder. If your bike has knobbly tyres but you mainly ride on the road, fit slicks and you will immediately notice an increase in handling, performance and speed. To boost speed, fit lighter tyres. If it's comfort you're after, fit a wider tyre – it's a lot cheaper than suspension and just as effective for riding on the road.

Wheels

You've sorted your tyres but you still want to squeeze out a bit more performance. Time for a set of lighter wheels. Decreasing the amount of rotating weight on your bike is the surest way to boost acceleration and climbing power – that's why the likes of Lance Armstrong ride bikes with the lightest wheels possible. You don't have to be a racer though to feel the benefit of a lighter wheel package: tourers, commuters and leisure riders can all benefit, but if you go lighter remember not to sacrifice too much strength.

Saddle

Whatever type of riding you do, comfort is key, particularly at that most important of all the contact points between you and your bike – the one you sit on. Saddles are a very personal thing, but the general rule is that the faster you ride and the more stretched your riding position, the narrower your saddle; the slower you ride and the more upright your riding position, the wider your saddle. Some women get on fine with men's saddles but many don't, so we'd advise most women to try a women's specific saddle. Aside from that you can choose from saddles with holes, saddles with grooves, even saddles with rivets. Softer is not necessarily better nor is it more expensive. If your current saddle is causing you problems it's really worth getting some advice from a good bike shop.

Clipless pedals

Aside from your wheels the most effective way to boost your cycling efficiency is to fit some clipless pedals and some shoes to match. Cleats in the bottom of the shoes attach you to the pedal, which means that you can pull the pedals up as well as push down. There are loads of different systems but most people are best off with a pair of double sided pedals as they're easier to get in and out of and the cleats recess into the shoes making them a lot easier to walk in than the single-sided systems favoured by road racers. Being attached to the bike may sound daunting, but with a little practice pedal entry and exit become second nature.

Suspension seatpost

Maybe your bike already has wider high volume tyres and you want even more comfort, or maybe you don't want to sacrifice performance by fitting wider tyres or a suspension fork but you still want a bit of cushion. A suspension seatpost (below) could well be the answer – it'll take the sting out of bad roads and even light trails without adding loads of weight to your bike.

Cycle storage

Do you have more bikes than room to store them in?

There's never enough space: that's rule number one of storing bikes. Rule number two is that your bike collection will expand to fit the space available.

Whether you live in a caravan or a mansion, you'll still have to use what space you've got effectively. Your bike storage needs to be convenient, secure and weatherproof. It also needs to be relatively innocuous. Your spouse or landlord may take exception to scraping their shins on pedals or mopping oily drips off the carpet.

In a one-room flat

Studio flats are often much smaller than the estate agent's patter suggests, but some are truly tiny. If you're renting it may be forbidden to start drilling holes in the walls, while fire regulations generally prevent you from using the corridor outside. You'll struggle to store more than a couple of conventional bikes in your room, however you do it.

Bike choice: Folding bike. The Brompton can be rolled under desks or into tight corners thanks to its little casters. If you want to be riding further afield, the Birdy packs down well.

How to store: Folders can go under the desk, at the end of the bed, in the wardrobe, by the door... Keep grime at bay by sitting them on strips of old carpet or cardboard. Two conventional solo bikes can be stored, without any drilling, using a stand or tower.

Access: Getting the bike outside or in again will be a grind, especially if you have to negotiate self-closing doors. If you have to climb stairs, it's easiest with a light bike carried cyclo-cross style on one shoulder. Keeping the bike clean will minimize grime on your hands/clothes.

Security: A bike stored behind a locked door will be covered by most household contents insurance policies (subject to the insurer's maximum bike pay-out which can be as low as £300). If you're not allowed to drill holes, lock the bike through the frame to something that won't easily go out of the door – such as the bed frame.

Note: If you're allowed to drill holes, you can use a bike hoist or wall-mounted storage hooks.

In a house

It's tempting simply to leave bikes in the hall, just inside the front door. While this is great for bike access, it can be awkward to get past the bikes if you're going out without one. This can be frustrating even for the cyclist, let alone anyone else.

Going up: Hallways often contain dead space above head height and this can be used for bike storage. All you need is a pulley-system, which you can either buy ready-made or create yourself using a couple of pulleys screwed into the ceiling (note that you'll need one double pulley as well as a single pulley, a couple of lengths of rope and a cleat in the wall to tie off the ropes). As well as using dead space, a hoist frees up space underneath in which you may be able to store another bike. You can also use two wall mounted hooks to store one bike above another in a hallway. It may seem odd to hook a bike just above floor level, but it won't move or fall over then, it'll keep the floor cleaner, and you may gain an anchor point for a lock.

The spare room: Any spare room can readily be used as a bike store, giving you as much room indoors – with heat as well as light – as a single garage. Obviously, ground floor rooms are best. However, a cellar makes a pretty good bike store/workshop. Use any combination of pulleys, wall hooks, free standing supports, etc. Even a small room such as an under-stair cupboard will probably fit a couple of bikes.

Security: Your bike should be fairly safe, as well as covered by your insurance, when it's in the house. But since you'll have a bike lock, you may as well use it. Fit a dedicated wall anchor or get a large ring-ended expander bolt from a hardware store. Do take your D-lock with you to the shop to make sure it fits through the ring.

Note: Don't fit carpet in any room used to store bikes. Linoleum or tiles are much easier to clean.

Outside

Lack of space inside may force you to store bikes outdoors, but there's a number of ways to protect your machine (or machines).

In the open air: At the very least fit a wall anchor (see page 92) so you can secure your bike to the house or a concrete floor; a wall is better in that it offers support. For weather protection, a PVC bike cover is better than nothing.

In a shed: A shed will keep the rain off your bike, but many are absurdly easy to break into. If the door can't be sprung open with a pry-bar, the thief can often unscrew the door at the hinges. Many sheds come with a raised wooden floor, which isn't what you want: you need to site the shed straight onto concrete so that you can embed wall anchors in the floor. If you lock one bike to the wall anchor and the other bikes to that bike, you might only need one anchor point. While some anchors will fit into wood, wooden sheds aren't tough enough to offer much security. If the shed has a window, cover it from the inside so the potential thief can't see what's in there.

A dedicated bike store: Unlike sheds, which you walk into, bike stores are only designed to hold bikes so they can fit into less space. They range from tinfoil-thick boxes up to business-style cycle lockers with four-figure price tags. We'd recommend supplementing its security – which isn't bad, to be honest – with concrete-floor-embedded 'wall' anchors (see page 92).

Note: Any padlock or D-lock that's exposed to the elements will need oiling at regular intervals to prevent it seizing up.

The garage

This is what non-garage owning cyclists dream of. You can now store as many bikes as you like! It's possible, but inconvenient, to lean them several deep against each other. Ideally you want to be able to access all of them, with the heaviest and most regularly used bikes sited so they're easiest to get at.

Wall hooks: You can buy simple plastic-coated bike hooks cheaply, but specialist hooks tend to be a lot sturdier, and as they stick out further – i.e. half or more the width of your bike's handlebars – they offer the option of hanging the bike by the top tube.

Wheel supports: These can be divided into two groups: those that support the bike by the wheel – like the butterfly-racks you get in old-style bike sheds – and those that hang the bike from the wheel. Since a bike wheel is much stronger concentrically than it is laterally, we prefer the latter. Hanging bikes vertically will get the most bikes into the least space (especially if you hang the bikes front wheel, back wheel, front wheel etc.), but they will of course stick out from the wall by the height of the bike. And it's slightly harder to get them on and off the rack compared to hanging them by the top tube.

Security: If your rack (or racks) won't allow a lock to be fitted, don't forget wall anchors (see page 92). Garages are more substantial than sheds, but often aren't much harder to break into. If there's more than one way into the garage, fit bolts to the bottom of the up-and-over door. Consider getting an alarm system too. (see also page 92).

Note: If there isn't any power in your garage, invest in a head torch. Careful use of hooks allows you to make the most of limited storage.

Home security

You wouldn't leave your bike unprotected from thieves on the street, but what about protecting it at home?

Ground/wall anchors

Ground/wall anchors provide a fixed point to lock your bike to. They are ideal for garages and sheds with solid (brick/concrete) walls or floors, and are the perfect companion to a good-quality chain lock.

Make sure that the shackle/hoop is tough enough to withstand attack and that the fixings are either hidden or defended. Usually the Allen head bolts will also be supplied with steel balls to hammer into the bolt's heads, so that it's impossible to undo them with Allen keys or drivers.

Also ensure that where it is fitted is where you want it to stay permanently, as once bolted down you won't be able to move it.

Finally, think about its position: if it's going to get in the way, try and get one where the shackle can be flattened, so as not to cause a trip hazard or prevent you getting your car into the garage.

Hasps and staples

It's all well and good having a top-rated lock inside your shed or garage, but ideally you should try to stop the thieves getting in at all. Look for a hasp with hidden fittings and a substantial thickness of metal on the padlock eye. If it's a garage you're securing, consider garage door defenders.

Alarms

If your shed/garage is without power there are plenty of battery alarms. Usually they are passive infrared sensors with 4^1/$_2$–6 metres (15–20 feet) range with between a 100 degree (wall mounted) and 360 degree sweep and a key fob remote. They can be loud (over 130 decibels), but do tend to consume batteries so if you intend to use one consider getting some rechargeable batteries at the same time.

Protecting accessories

A big chain and floor or wall mount is going to hold the bulk of your bike, but those expensive extras are going to still be vulnerable, so buy flexible cable to thread through wheels, saddles, chainsets etc.

Another great tip is that if you have more than one bike to lock, thread the cables between the two bikes. Low or high, these can become a trip hazard to any potential thief and at least make it very difficult for them to move around your bike.

Ground anchor (right), padlock and shed alarm (opposite).

See page 140

Chain locks

Chains are the ultimate way to lock your bike, although their weight (up to 8kg (17lb)) means they aren't very portable. They are perfect for home (or to leave at work) and combined with a good anchor they're the best way to keep your bike(s) secure.

Padlocks

As with hasps, this is your first line of defence. Look for shrouded shackles and hardened steel construction, plus plenty of key combinations. Buy the very best you can afford.

Top tip

Ideally use more than one security device – particularly if you keep your bike in a shed – and use products from different manufacturers: for instance an Abus chain with a Magnum lock. Thieves have particular tools and methods of attack for different types of lock: giving them different makes to beat makes things a lot harder – especially for pickers.

Lock maintenance

It's all well and good buying and using the toughest lock you can find to keep things safe at home, but what happens if something goes wrong? Yes you will be able to remove the lock with the help of brute force and some expensive power tools, or the employ of a decent locksmith, but prevention is better than the cure: think about where the lock is to be used – your average shed, garage or outbuilding will be subject to the elements – namely damp in the winter and humidity in the summer. Neither of these are ideal for lock mechanisms so we'd recommend a regular dousing with a water displacing lube (WD40) and then a light lube as this will also help stop surface corrosion. Another monthly tip is to spray the key with lube and lock and unlock the mechanism a few times so the lube gets deep into the mechanics of the lock. This should keep it working smoothly for years.

Careful now!

We can't stress enough the importance of being careful with chainlocks. Some of the locks weigh in excess of 5kg (10lbs), which is pretty substantial, and if you drop it onto a lightweight racing frame it's going to leave a mark. So use both hands, and drape the chain through the frame gently then hold both ends before attaching the padlock and lower the lock down, do not just let it go – no matter how much of a hurry you may be in – as a big dent in your favourite race bike is going to ruin your day!

Secondary security

1 Ensure that all of your hand tools, power tools, toolbox etc. are all locked away securely with a good-quality padlock. If a thief manages to get into your property don't help them out by offering them all the tools they need to take your bike (or parts of it).
2 Make it difficult. Don't leave your bikes at the front of the shed so they're the first thing a thief will see – make it awkward by leaving stuff in the way: boxes, cans, whatever. This may seem a chore when you add five minutes to your commute getting your bike out, but remember if it's a pain for you it's going to be difficult for a thief too, and if you don't have an alarm fitted, the idiot stumbling over oil cans, lawn mowers etc. is going to be making some serious noise.

What do Sold Secure and Thatcham mean?

Both Sold Secure and Thatcham test their locks using thieves' own methods. Sold Secure use a three-tier standard to test their locks – gold, silver and bronze (see page 57). Thatcham's locks are designed for motorbikes, but for heavy duty, top-level security they work just as well on bikes. 'We don't have grades, the lock either passes or it doesn't and it must resist for five minutes,' said Martyn Randle, research engineer for Thatcham.

Another check is to make sure the key has a sufficient number of combinations, unlike cheaper locks which only have about ten, so that thieves can't try a selection of keys to open the lock.

Security and insurance for bikes

Take all the precautions you can – bikes are always a target.

As the majority of bicycle thefts are opportunistic, it is essential that you always lock your bike, even if you are just leaving it for a matter of seconds (see also pages 54–57). It is also advisable to store it securely and lock it even while at home (see page 90–93). But if your bike is stolen, what can you do to help get it back, how should you report it to the police, and will it be covered on your insurance?

Security measures

To help you get your bike back if it is stolen there are a few things that you can do. First, make sure you have security marked your bike. If your bike is found then you will not only be able to prove that it is yours, but it improves the chances of it being returned to you. A thief may also find that it is harder to sell a bike that is security marked, so may avoid stealing it if there is an option of an easier to market steed.

Electronic tagging devices will also not prevent your bike from being taken, but will make it more likely that you will get it back. Again, make it obvious that your bike is tagged so that this is a deterrent to thieves.

Reporting theft

Always report bicycle theft to the police. Even if you think it's unlikely they will recover your bike, it is worth reporting it. Try to provide as much information as you can, including the frame number, type of bike, if possible a photograph, and of course details of where and when it was stolen.

Crime figures are an important measure for the police and can influence how they distribute their resources. To report a theft online you can go to www.online.police.uk, or contact your local police station – you can report either by phone or in person.

When you report the theft ask for your CAD (Computer Aided Despatch) or CRIS (Crime Reference Information System) number. Having a number will help you to track the progress of your case.

If you have theft insurance you will need to report the theft to your insurance company or insurance broker. Bear in mind that, while some insurance companies are happy with a police crime number, others will require the broken lock and your key.

Insuring bikes

Let's say, for example, that you own a bike that is worth over £1,000. It's locked in the house most of the time and you use it for commuting to work where it's locked outside to an immovable object, like a bike rack, using a Sold Secure or Thatcham rated lock. If you do all this you will meet the security requirements of the CTC's bike insurance Cyclecover, British Cycling and Evans Cycles Insurance, Cycleguard and Churchill. All these companies cover theft, damage and malicious damage, plus if you're forced off your bike and it's stolen you will be covered. But how much do they cost? And what does each offer? See page 138 for contact information.

Note: With all insurance policies, make sure you read the terms and conditions. For example, for racing be aware that some companies only cover time trialling. Prices also vary depending on where you live, previous claims, where the bike is kept and what it's used for.

Taking out insurance

Always carefully check the small print on your cycle insurance – it may not be all you thought.

You've put a lot of time and effort into buying yourself a decent bicycle and you've taken the sensible precaution of insuring it. You've checked out the policy and found one that covers theft and accidental damage in both the home and in transit, say to and from events, or en route to your holiday destination. Like most cyclists you own an estate car or perhaps an MPV such as a Renault Espace. You stop overnight at a motor lodge, or for lunch at a roadside café. You've taken the sensible precautions of covering your cycle(s) with blankets, etc., and perhaps even locked them within the vehicle. Modern society being what it is, your vehicle is broken into and your beloved cycle(s) stolen. You contact your insurance broker who then informs you that you are not covered. The cycle must be in a 'locked boot' which is independent of the main body of the vehicle and cannot be accessed from the car interior – so that means theft from all estate cars, MPVs, SUVs, hatchbacks and the majority of saloon cars is not covered. Crazily, if you'd had them locked onto an exterior rack they would have been covered – but you wouldn't be so irresponsible as to leave your baby out in the open all night, would you?

This is a true incident and is the general case with many insurers. So make sure that you check your policy carefully and phone for clarification if you are in any doubt as to what you are covered for.

As is the case with home contents insurance, where you live will to an extent determine the size of your cycle insurance premium. Residents in areas that have a high level of bicycle thefts, typically cities, can expect to pay slightly more for their cover.

Whilst cycling is overwhelmingly seen to have health benefits, accidents do happen and if you regularly cycle on busy routes it may be sensible to extend your insurance cover accordingly as the principal danger for cyclists is other road users! See pages 106–16 for more information on road safety. There are two additional insurance options to consider.

Third Party Cover

Whilst mandatory for drivers, cyclists are not legally required to have third party cover. However if you are cited by another road user for causing injury to their person or damage to their property, and this claim is upheld, you could face significant costs. Third party cover will offer you valuable protection against this and many insurance companies will be able to offer this service alongside a basic cycling policy.

Personal Accident Cover

Similarly, if you are injured whilst riding, personal accident cover will provide benefits for hospital treatment, permanent disability or death. Again this could be arranged by your existing insurers though there may be some significant exceptions, such as competitive cycling, which may need to be dealt with separately.

Some of the large cycling organisations, including the LCC, CTC and British Cycling, offer insurance services for their members which provide specialist and comprehensive cover, often at a discounted rate.

Even if you are extremely careful about your bike's security, do think about times when you may not be covered by your insurance policy.

Cycle training courses

Brush up on your road safety skills, or learn the basics before going taking to the streets

Why should I take a training course?

Learning how to cycle properly makes cycling much more enjoyable and safer for everyone – children, adults and other road users. There are many reasons why someone misses out on learning to ride a bike safely in traffic but the great thing is that you are never too old to learn! Some beginners have previously had bad experiences whilst trying to learn that have left them feeling fearful about falling and without any confidence in their ability to learn the skill of cycling.

Whatever your level, it is worth checking to see if there is a suitable course – whether you want to acquire new skills and techniques, to increase your confidence, help you train for a challenging ride, commute to work or school or to help you look after your bike.

Previously training was only available to children and was operated by Local Authorities in schools. Now cycling and road safety organisations have joined together with the Department for Transport and Cycling England to create a new National Standard for Cycle Training. There are training courses nationwide for both adults and children, based in real traffic scenarios under safe supervision.

What will I learn?

The National Standard for Cycle Training is a three tier training scheme:

Level 1 – Conducted in a controlled environment away from roads and traffic. Cyclists are usually trained in groups of 3–12 riders, although individual training may be available. Provides the basic cycle control skills including, starting and pedalling, stopping, manoeuvring, signalling and using the gears.
Level 2 – On-road training for those who have completed Level 1 and are ready to progress; it gives real cycling experience and makes trainees feel safer and capable of dealing with traffic on short commuting journeys or when cycling to school. Training is mainly in small groups over a number of sessions.
Level 3 – Develops the basic skills and trains riders to make journeys in a variety of traffic conditions competently, confidently and consistently. Cyclists

reaching the Level 3 standard will be able to deal with all types of road conditions and more complex situations. The course covers dealing with hazards, making 'on-the-move' risk assessments and planning routes for safer cycling.

Courses can also include training for cycling at night, security, luggage and load carrying and using your bike with public transport.

By the end of the training you should be starting to feel confident about making cycle journeys in a variety of traffic conditions.

Costs

Training can cost from £15 per person per session, depending on your location. Many local authorities fund courses that are free or subsidised.

Find a course

The best place to start looking for local courses and instructors is the CTC. They can offer a range of advice, including which course would be suitable for you. Call the Cycle Training Hotline on 0870 607 04 5 or visit www.ctc.org.uk

A cycle course can give you the confidence and skills you need before taking on the traffic.

One commuter's experience

I'm the first to arrive at the Faster Commuter course, run by Cycle Training UK in London. CTUK, a not-for-profit company started in 1998 and now run as a co-operative, bills itself as the largest provider of independent cycle training in Britain. They aim to pollinate the country with competent, confident cyclists – much of their work is with children. By the end of the one-day course 'trainees should be more confident, self-reliant cyclists able to deal with a wide range of conditions.'

We start with breakfast: porridge oats and orange juice. Frightfully healthy, it's the opening salvo of the curriculum: fast commuters need quality fuel.

Next we dive into the alphabet. The 'M-Check' is a 'systematic approach minimizing the possibility of missing faults', which starts with the front hub and wheel, climbs up to the handlebars, scoots down to the bottom bracket, back up to the saddle and ends at the rear, stopping at all potential trouble-spots in between. The lesson: safe bike = reliable transport = faster commuter.

We do a quick run-through of preventative maintenance, learn how to repair a puncture, etc., and prepare for a field trip. First our bicycles are checked for roadworthiness as we are briefed on control skills: emergency stops, changing gears, signalling and pothole manoeuvres. For the gear changing exercise we ride in a circle and click up or down while attempting to maintain a steady cadence, the holy grail of fast, unflustered commuters. My hand signals aren't 100 per cent kosher as I don't hold my palm perpendicular to the ground in CTUK-approved fashion, preferring a no-nonsense pointing finger. We spend some time practising looking over our shoulder while signalling, later adding a one-handed controlled stop. We end the session by running over a tool bag, pulling up on the handlebars as we should do if it were the pothole it represents.

After lunch we discuss desirable component upgrades and sensible choices in attire. Did you know that fluorescent materials lose their special powers at night because headlamps don't have the ultraviolet light they crave? Helmets are not a mandatory requirement for this or any CTUK course, although this stance makes them unpopular with many of the authorities they solicit as clients.

The tutors then conduct a thorough physiology lesson, touching on warm-up regimes and stretches, the glycogen window, and 'Fartlek', which is Swedish for 'speed play' and is interval training.

Then we are on the road again. 'Most people are a bad advert for cycling' my tutor comments. Chances are my shadow is not going to be pleased with some of my moves but the fact that I'm alive and pedalling after years of coexisting peacefully with the rest of London traffic is my testament that I must be doing something right. My chief failing appears to be not positioning myself for optimum visibility, spending too much time in secondary riding position. Guilty as charged on this occasion: I see nothing wrong with allowing faster traffic to pass. Actual kerb hugging is denounced in no uncertain terms by many safety experts, including John Franklin in Cyclecraft. I sometimes inhabit the car door zone but have never been 'doored' because I have eyes like relentless minesweepers. I believe that you can be quite aware of your environment without being obvious about it.

After a T-junction tutorial we tackle busy roads and roundabouts. The roadie session is all too brief. Ian promises it will be expanded in future.

We end the day in a rush, with feedback forms quickly scribbled on. 'Overall, it was an interesting course,' writes Nicola. 'I'm sure that most of us did know it all, but at times it doesn't hurt to have that knowledge reinforced.' Rose is a fan of the CTUK/national standards approach to holding your lane and encouraging motorists to respect your space. However, this magic did not last when I was riding through central London with vehicles accelerating and moving fast, dodging around each other in the evening rush hour or after dark. In these circumstances there is little scope for communication, or control of the traffic, and the default has to be finding a way to get the hell out.

Go ride!

Once you have mastered the basics, getting around on busy streets is easy. The difficulty is in improving your skills and experience safely.

Don't expect it to be simple from the start – time invested in learning, and money spent on equipment and clothing, will be paid back a thousandfold once you're fully and freely mobile.

The knack of travelling by bike on roads shared with heavy flows of pushy traffic includes important technical elements – you need to be able to control your bike and understand the rules of traffic (see pages 102–104) – but traffic riding is essentially a social endeavour: you're sharing space with others. The hazard is not the road, not really even cars, trucks or buses, the hazards come from other people. Once you understand this you're halfway to becoming a safe and comfortable rider.

Control skills

If you're new to riding or coming back after a lay-off, begin by checking and polishing your control skills away from other traffic. Pay particular attention to stopping and starting. Riding a bike is not difficult, but it's very different from standing or walking – so don't try to mix riding and walking by scooting or shuffling. Either sit on your bike and ride it or get off and push.

Beginners need their seat set low enough so they can touch the ground easily while in the saddle. As take-offs and landings become routine you can wait standing across your bike – not sitting on the seat – and use the pedals to step up to the seat as you set off, and to climb down as you stop. Mastery of this technique will allow you to raise your seat so that pedalling is more comfortable and less of an effort.

A bike ridden at, or above, jogging pace is much easier to steer than one going at, or below, walking speed. When faced with a tricky situation the best options are either to stop or to keep going briskly – going forward slowly is often trickiest. Keeping your head up and looking ahead will help you stay in smooth, dynamic control.

You need to be able to ride one-handed to give bold and confident signals and to look over your shoulder to see what's going on behind. It's necessary to be vigilant and aware of what's going on all around but focus your attention on where you want to go, not on what you want to avoid. If you pay too much attention to obstacles they can draw you inexorably towards them.

Start riding on roads you're familiar with, when there's not too much busy traffic and where the junctions aren't too complex. You can work up to busier and bigger roads as your skill and confidence grows. Don't worry about walking across junctions you find difficult. It's better to walk a little of a journey than leave your bike at home. Take a little time to watch the traffic at places where you find problems. Which lane of traffic goes where? How do other people on bikes manage? You can learn from watching both the accomplished and the incompetent. You'll soon make progress and be riding where you used to walk.

If your bike has a choice of gears select those that allow your feet to spin without a lot of straining or pushing. This may feel strange at first – riding a bike is definitely not natural – but once you get used to it, it's much less effort and better for your bike and body. On the road it's easier to adjust your speed when your legs are spinning freely, and harder to accelerate or slow down if you're struggling to keep the pedals turning.

Practise making sudden stops to get a feeling of how much space you need in different weather conditions and on different road surfaces. Use both brakes and hold your weight back with your arms. In emergency braking you're looking for the point just before the back wheel locks and skids. Check your bike carefully, or show it to an experienced rider or take it to a shop. Confidence in your machine and your bike-handling skills will make traffic riding much more pleasant.

Social skills: The art of cycling in traffic

On congested roads when people, desperate to keep moving in cars, buses and trucks, meet someone on a bike they often see them not as a fellow traveller but as an opportunity to capture some precious space. They may try to bully you out of your priority by – for example – creeping out of side roads into your path, or perhaps drifting into the lane you're using, offering unspoken threats, 'Oh no, I can't see you'. It's important to understand that this behaviour is not a danger but a deliberate bluff. It may well be frightening at first but only because these people – perhaps

without thinking what they're doing – are trying to frighten you.

If you meet this intimidation with a confident manner – 'this is my right of way and I intend to use it' – the seeming hazard evaporates. You have to watch out for the one in 10,000 who's actually asleep, has looked where you are and seen an empty road. This slight risk makes a good understanding of your emergency braking distance important. Take this distance, add a margin for error – save riding at 100 per cent for the racetrack – then ride purposefully towards the space where you have priority.

The rules of the road

Make sure you understand the rules of traffic before you go onto the road, especially if you don't have experience of driving a car or riding a motorcycle.

Consider getting a copy of The Highway Code (see page 115) – most newsagents sell it – but remember it explains how things are supposed to be, not exactly how they are in real life...

Even on a busy street corner you might wait months to see two cars bump, which reveals how formal the system is. The person who doesn't follow the 'rules' is very rare and you can usually spot them coming from a long way off. Traffic mostly behaves in very predictable ways but you won't find these rules written down, you have to study them on the streets and they may vary from town to town or even in different districts of the same city.

Junctions

Getting in the right position early and dealing with one issue at a time is important at junctions. It is worth bearing in mind that sometimes – if, for example, you are in heavy traffic – your best option may be to get off and walk! **(FIG 1)**.

When turning right into a side road the first element is crossing the carriageway you're in. Look behind early, signal right if need be – when it's safe – make a diagonal move to take a position just to the left of the road's centre-line.

Now you've dealt with any potential conflict with traffic going in the same direction as you – which can pass on your left, if there's room, or stay behind until you turn – you can concentrate on looking for a gap in the oncoming traffic. Try to time your arrival at the junction to coincide with a gap in this traffic. If not, you'll have to wait in the middle of the road. This may seem exposed but it is where all road users are most watchful.

Once there's a gap in oncoming traffic take a quick look over your right shoulder, then cross the oncoming carriageway into the side road, looking out for traffic emerging from the side road. A square turn, from a point in line with your position in the road you're entering, gets you across the opposite carriageway

quickest and reduces the risk of conflict with traffic coming out of the road you're turning into **(FIG 2)**.

Position on the road

Riding safely on the road involves controlling the space around you. An important element is to consider 'where on the road shall I ride?' Positioning is not an exact science – there's often more than one 'correct' answer, but it's important to be definite, don't drift. Ask yourself: Where will I get an easy and unobstructed passage? Where can I see and be seen? What does my position tell others about what I'm planning to do?

Beginners often try to 'keep out of the way' because they don't want to be a nuisance, and end up riding too close to parked cars or the edge of the road. This is dangerous because it makes it more likely that other people won't see you. Everyone using the road looks where they're going and almost always where they expect other traffic to be. If you can be seen you're safe. Successful riders don't try and keep out of the way of traffic – they are part of the traffic. Be courteous and helpful – by using your bike you're already doing everyone a favour – but take enough space to make sure others notice you.

The first position to consider is the centre of the leftmost lane of moving traffic **(FIG 3)**. Here you are safe from any swinging car doors, you're easy to see and have a better view around obstacles and into side roads. If potentially faster traffic is building up behind and the road ahead is clear you can choose to move to the left to help them overtake, but only if safe to do so. There's no point letting traffic squeeze through if there isn't room to pass safely or if it's going to block the road a few yards ahead.

Always take a quick look behind before you change your position on the road. On a busy road you should have a good idea of what's going on behind, but don't look back for too long or you may miss hazards developing ahead.

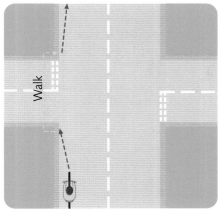

FIG 1

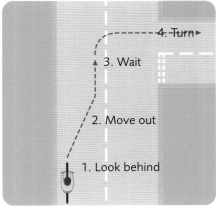

FIG 2

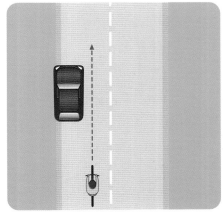

FIG 3

Dealing with congestion

Never try to pass between a truck and the kerb (FIG 4). If a truck is behind you take the middle of the lane to prevent it passing you without changing lanes. If a truck is waiting ahead of you don't try to overtake it unless you are certain you can get safely past before it starts moving. When following a truck stay in a place where the driver can see you. Watch the wing mirrors. If you can't see the driver he or she can't see you.

When you meet congestion the safest option is to join the queue in the middle of the leftmost lane or – when approaching a junction – in the appropriate lane for the direction you're going (FIG 5). This will stop other vehicles pulling alongside you and causing turning conflicts.If you want to avoid delay, and the opposite carriageway is clear, another choice is to overtake the queue on the right.

Don't speed, and be aware of refuge space on the left side of the centreline in case oncoming traffic appears. If you do cross into the other carriageway go far enough over to be visible and safe from vehicles leaving the queue with a sudden 'U' turn. When you reach the front you can use an Advance Stop Line (ASL) refuge if there is one, otherwise take care how you rejoin the waiting traffic. When 'jumping' the queue where there is no ASL, it is often safest to integrate behind the first vehicle in the queue. Take a position where everyone can see you.

If you decide to move ahead on the inside of stationary motor-traffic, either against the kerb or between files of vehicles, go slowly, and watch out for opening doors or pedestrians crossing. If congestion means you have to pass parked cars in the zone where you might be hit by an opened door slow down to walking pace. Long lorries pose a particular hazard for cyclists.

Separating hazard and conflict

Aim to deal with hazards and conflicts one at a time. For example if you're riding along in the kerb lane and see it's blocked by a car parked ahead, the car is a hazard because it narrows the road and obstructs sight lines. There's also potential for conflict with any faster traffic using the next lane because you have to move into this lane to pass the parked car. The first thing you need to do is look behind, then if necessary give a right signal and – when safe to do so – make a shallow diagonal move to a position that will allow you to pass the car clear of its door zone.

It's important to complete the move from one lane to the next – and thus resolve any potential conflict – before you near the hazard. It's much more difficult and dangerous to get around the parked car if you leave the rightward move too late and change lanes immediately behind the parked car. From here you're trying to deal with the hazard and the conflict together (FIG 6).

Roundabouts

Roundabouts can often pose a considerable hazard to cyclists. The Highway Code advises cyclists to either keep to the left or to dismount and walk around. When negotiating roundabouts it is important to remember that drivers entering and exiting may be concentrating more on the other traffic and may be less likely to notice cyclists. Be aware at all times, especially when cycling across exits – you may need to signal right to show you are not leaving the roundabout. Also be aware of vehicles that need to cross your path to enter or exit the roundabout. Give plenty of room to long vehicles as they need more space to manoeuvre.

Many roundabouts have a crossing soon after the exit, or just before an entry. These are not always visible from the main junction. Be aware that there may be a red light as you turn off the roundabout, and be prepared to stop.

Cycle lanes

There are various types of cycle lane and it is essential to understand how they are all supposed to function.

Mandatory cycle lanes are identified by a solid white line. These are for cyclists only – other vehicles are prohibited from entering them. Advisory cycle lanes are identified by a broken white line. They are partly open to other vehicles – only when it is safe to enter. Advanced stop lines are the green boxes on the road, placed at the front of traffic light junctions with a cycle lane leading up to them. They allow cyclists to position themselves at the front of traffic, ensuring they are in full view. These are designed to make it easier and safer to proceed from the junction. You may also end up sharing your cycle lane with pedestrians – often on the paths that run through parks.

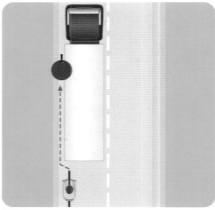

FIG 4

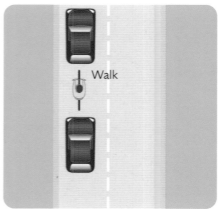

Walk

FIG 5

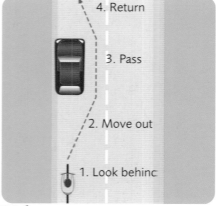

4. Return

3. Pass

2. Move out

1. Look behind

FIG 6

Road safety

The principal danger when cycling to work is other traffic.

Although some drivers are reckless, most are considerate, and almost none malicious. Junctions are flash points for accidents, accounting for 70 per cent of motor vehicle/cyclist collisions. Roundabouts, slip roads, crossroads and private drives are potentially hazardous, but the most dangerous, statistically, are T-junctions. The biggest risk at a T-junction is when a car emerges from a side road and hits the cyclist travelling on the main carriageway.

The problem is one of awareness – or lack of it. Drivers either don't see you at all or fail to understand your intentions. Make them. Ride confidently and predictably. Signal boldly. Eyeball drivers. Whenever you're not sure what a driver is going to do, assume the worst unless the evidence tells you otherwise. In short, if you act like traffic, you'll be treated like traffic (see also pages 102–104). And don't forget that the health benefits of regular cycling do outweigh the risks, according to the British Medical Association.

Road surfaces are sometimes a danger. In particular, look out for tram tracks, drain covers and shiny tarmac sealing lines – especially when wet. Potholes are less of a problem. Either move out in advance if you know one's there, or rise up on the pedals to unweight the bike and roll through it; it's safer than swerving suddenly.

Punctures happen fairly rarely. A moderately tough tyre, properly inflated, will often shrug off broken glass. If you're riding in an area where hedge cuttings are common, use Slime or a similar product on your inner tubes. And always carry a pump, a spare tube and any tools you need to fit it (see pages 60–61).

The statistics

Government departments, cyclists' pressure groups and independent analysts all produce their own data on cycling safety issues and all argue with each other about what the figures mean. Are the roads safer for cyclists than ten years ago? Which roads are the most dangerous? What group of cyclists is most at risk? To the ordinary cyclist on the street – or cycle path – this can be confusing to say the least.

Statistics seem most confusing of all, and whoever produces them can be open to the accusation of producing figures that suit their agenda. This isn't to say that there isn't much valuable statistical study and that earnest analysis cannot help to make the cycling world a better place, just that we should also think about where figures come from and why they have been produced.

Where the figures come from

Government figures may come from their own statistics departments or from the Office for National Statistics or they may be commissioned and produced by research bodies such as TRL Limited (which has a huge transport library and many testing facilities). Many of these are helpful, the product of long hours of work – the problem with inaccurate or misleading statistics can come when quoted out of context and in isolation or if we don't know how the figures were actually arrived at. There are also independent analysts working as individuals in the area of cycle safety who are often critical of government figures, claims and official policies.

Government statistics are collected from a variety of sources. The government itself is mainly concerned with cycle traffic on the public road network and uses both traffic enumerators, who sit and count traffic on selected roads, and the National Travel Survey. The 'NTS' is based on the 'travel diaries' of – and interviews with – randomly selected households. Government bicycle accident statistics generally originate from police paperwork as the police are obliged to fill in given details for accidents on the road involving personal injury.

Cycling organizations also produce statistics and reports. Sustrans has an ongoing programme of monitoring along twenty-two National Cycle Network routes, headed by an expert in transport statistics. Surveys were carried out in the field, and automatic bike counters have also been used.

But statistics can only show part of the picture. The figures are based on samples and cannot give a

100 per cent accurate picture of the real situation – most problematic is the fact that many government figures for cycling only include road trips. Traffic-free data as compiled mainly by Sustrans is in its infancy and so long-term trends have yet to emerge.

Where are you safest?

Trying to assess how risky riding on the road is depends on what you compare it to. Fatalities and serious injuries to road cyclists have declined steadily over recent years and massively over the last fifty years. However, much of this decline reflects the fact that over time there have been fewer and fewer cyclists on the road.

In 2000 there were 127 reported cycling fatalities on the roads and 2,643 serious cyclist injuries. This shows a significant decrease from 1999, but cycling on the roads itself declined so these figures themselves don't seem to say too much. However, government figures from 1994–2000 state that, per 100 million vehicle kilometres (62 million vehicle miles) cycled, the total casualty rate has fallen from 572 to 509 and within this the killed and seriously injured figure has fallen from 88 to 68, suggesting that in real terms the roads have become 10–20 per cent safer (or that cyclists are riding more safely). Compared to other road users, figures and common sense tell us cyclists are more at risk: car user casualty rates are some ten times lower at around 55 per 100 million vehicle kilometers (62 million vehicle miles). (Based on: Road Accidents GB 2000: The Casualty Report.)

What's being done to make the roads safer

- The Bad Driving Offences Consultation is calling for greater penalties for offenders and is looking at how to categorize traffic crimes. 'One thing the government is worried about is that this will take more court time and prison space. But this is no excuse, people who are a danger to society should be given the proper penalties,' said Adam Coffmann, Senior Transport Campaigner for the CTC.
- The Safer Streets Coalition, involving 29 members including Sustrans and the CTC, aims to make roads in Britain safer by imposing speed limits and acting against mobile phone use, jumping red lights and drink driving.

Roads vs cycle lanes

Because the National Cycle Network traffic-free sections and the road system are monitored separately and in different ways there is no direct comparison as to which is safer and small-scale studies can be notoriously misleading. One analyst's figures for the Redway system of Milton Keynes put serious injuries to cyclists on the Redways at 23 over a decade compared to 21 on the road system. York, however, one of the UK's leading cycle cities, boasts figures that suggest cycle tracks and lanes have contributed to cycling levels and safety. Since the mid-1980s a 72km (45 mile) network of cycle tracks has been introduced and the decline of the number of cycling trips made in a city with traditionally high cycling levels has been halted at around 21 per cent of all trips. The city has achieved a one-third reduction in traffic accidents. Again though, the figures are only part of the debate, simply raising questions about whether cyclists are being 'forced' off the road onto not always ideal cycle paths or whether new facilities will make things safer and encourage cycling.

Keep it in proportion

Living involves risk and it seems, in the overall scheme of things to worry about, dangers to cyclists comes a long way down the list.

Of course there are massive benefits which for many will far outweigh any perceived danger – much reporting in the 'non-cycling' media and many government pronouncements seem to infer that cycling is inherently dangerous (clearly nonsense – as seasoned cyclists know, rider skill, behaviour, choice of route and experience are major factors in how dangerous you make cycling for yourself).

The British Medical Association, for example, although showing concern about road safety issues and being pro compulsory helmet wear, still advocates cycling as a way of improving life expectancy. A survey based on Office of Population Census data in 1986 showed that relative to cycling (index 1), fatality indices for other sports and leisure activities were tennis 4.2, football 4.9, swimming 7, horse riding 29, fishing 41, climbing 137 and airsports 450. Only golf at 0.83 and rambling at 0.06 were safer according to the study. A Danish mortality study in 2000 found that cycling (average three hours per week) led to the lowest mortality rate of all activities in everyday life. So keep cycling and you'll be a healthier individual seems to be the overall message of the figures.

The solicitor's view

Alyson France is a solicitor specializing in acting for cyclists involved in personal injury cases.
See www.bikeline.co.uk

Q What do you think would contribute most to reducing serious accidents for cyclists?

A I have always believed that the only long-term way in which accidents to cyclists (and pedestrians) could be reduced is educating those motorists that need it, not to see cyclists as an obstruction but as legitimate road users who are helping, not hindering, the congestion/pollution situation.

Q Where are the most dangerous places to cycle?

A The roads! But that doesn't mean that we should avoid riding on them. The emphasis being placed on cycle paths these days worries me – is this just the first step to banning us from the roads completely? Put in context though, I don't think cycling on the roads is dangerous. The number of serious injuries I deal with are relatively few. Out of about 275–300 cases a year, I only have one fatal and three very serious accidents. Of the remainder, about 20 per cent have fractures of some kind, although not serious, with the rest having soft-tissue injuries. Still too many, but reassuring enough to keep me on my bike.

Q Where do you stand on the great helmet debate?

A I am very firmly against compulsory helmet use. I remain to be convinced that helmets can have the universal safety benefits of motorcycle helmets (and yes, I am a motorcyclist!), and be light and comfortable enough to wear. It is not the lack of a helmet that causes most cyclist injuries – it's the carelessness of motorists.

Q What class of cyclists is most at risk?

A I'm not sure that any particular class of cyclists are at risk. My clients range from top internationals out training to dinner ladies on shopping bikes riding to work. However, some experienced cyclists may be better at 'defensive riding'.

The expert's view

John Franklin is an expert witness and author of 'Cyclecraft', the cycling equivalent of the police Roadcraft manual. See www.lesberries.co.uk/cycling

Q What do you think would contribute most to reducing serious accidents for cyclists?

A Restricting motor vehicle performance (i.e. rate of acceleration but also braking) at the design stage, a matter for European legislation. That could considerably calm the roads and make it easier for everyone to exercise better judgement.

Q Where are the most dangerous places to cycle?

A That depends to an extent on the person. In absolute terms, the most dangerous places are where there is a moderate amount of traffic (it's safer where it's congested), high speeds and complex weaving movements. Some (but overall only a minority of) roundabouts and gyratories fall into this category, particularly in outer urban areas and at motorway junctions.

Q Where do you stand on the great helmet debate?

A On the need for better information to enable people to make a more informed judgment. To some people the wearing of helmets has become an end in itself rather than a means to an end, which has largely been lost sight of. Meanwhile thousands of people are being scared off cycling, and missing out on huge health benefits, by the false perception that head injury among cyclists is common and inevitable.

Q What class of cyclists is most at risk?

A Novice cyclists (including children) lack control skills and are most likely to fall off, but the group that's most likely to suffer serious injury involving another vehicle is probably a couple of stages more advanced than that. They've largely (but not completely) mastered control skills and probably think of themselves as reasonably competent, but they have not yet gained sufficient experience to deal with situations they haven't met before.

Know your rights

Like every other road user, cyclists have rights and responsibilities when it comes to the law.

Most motorists are aware of what happens if they break the law – they're looking at penalty points, fines, and even prison. There is a routine to follow in the event of a car 'bump' involving swapping insurance details and getting witness names. But how many cyclists know exactly what to do in the event of a crash or a road rage incident? Do you know what condition your bike should be in by law? Are you aware of your rights and obligations on the road? Sadly, accidents will happen, so it's important you know your rights.

Dealing with road rage

In conflict situations where you have right of way it's important to decide quickly whether to defer or enforce your priority. If you decide to defer, the crucial thing is not to get angry, so all the surrender costs is the short time it takes, and any energy needed to re-accelerate. If you choose to keep going and exercise your priority be bold and clear. The thing to avoid is uncertainty, which can escalate to the point where a motorist's formal demonstration of threat starts to become a real danger.

It's not your job to show people they're wrong and you're right, or to try and teach them to behave better – all you have to do is get where you want to go with the minimum of stress. Practise being forceful without being angry.

A bell can be very useful when you're being pushy, but if you're at risk a shout is better. A bold warning can be useful for confirming whether other people are trying a bluff or have really overlooked your presence.

Don't rush your journeys; it's easy to get infected by the pushy attitude that strikes people struggling to move motor-vehicles.

Don't fall for the victim mentality. Conditions for cycling may not be perfect but it's still the healthiest, most reliable and entertaining way to get around. Remember how lucky you are. Smile and be kind to other people even when their behaviour is immature and selfish. It's the best way to tempt them to follow your example.

What to do in the event of a collision with a motor vehicle

The following assumes you have had any necessary medical treatment on the spot (see also page 116) and have made sure you are fit to take these steps – your health comes first!

- Don't admit it was your fault.
- Make a note of the driver's name, address, insurance details and registration number but otherwise say as little as possible.
- Try to enlist the help of witnesses to the accident and get their contact details.
- Report the incident to the police. You are legally obliged to do so if there is any injury to people.
- See a doctor as soon as possible to get an assessment of any injuries – even if you feel alright.
- Get some legal advice as soon as possible.
- Get photographic evidence of any injuries and, if practical, of the incident site.
- Make a written account of exactly what happened as soon as you are able to.

Be civil about it

A minor accident might turn your mind to making a claim against the other party involved – particularly in these days of law firm television advertisements and company representatives roaming shopping precincts asking passers-by if they've ever had an accident.

If you make a claim against another person you are in the arena of civil law. This is not concerned with punishment for a criminal act but with protecting your rights against another person or organization.

The legal system, either through lawyers or civil court proceedings, must determine whose fault (liability) an accident is. Accidents are not always said to be totally the fault of one side or the other – you might find yourself being told you are 30 per cent to blame. Accidents involving serious injury and/or criminal prosecutions can also be the subject of a civil claim.

Generally, you can claim damages for physical injury and

damage to your bike plus legal costs and certain other expenses such as loss of earnings should you win the case. Often the claim doesn't get to court, being settled by the driver's insurers in the case of a collision with a motor vehicle. If you hit or are hit by a pedestrian any claim is much less certain and often depends on the insurance position (see page 112).

It goes without saying that you should always try to cycle within the law and the rules of the road – any criminal conviction of a cyclist, motorist or pedestrian, although a separate matter, can be used as evidence of fault in a civil case where the burden of proof is actually lower – fault must be established on the balance of probability, not beyond reasonable doubt as in criminal cases.

You cannot claim damages unless you have sustained physical injury or damage to your bike, although damages can be awarded for mental trauma if it accompanies any injury.

If you have a 'close shave' or are cut up you can take the driver's registration number and report the matter to the police but without witnesses you are unlikely to get very far. In a similar situation with public buses, council vehicles or company vehicles you can report the behaviour to the organization.

Crime doesn't pay

Unlike civil law, criminal law is concerned with what are seen as wrongs against society and where guilt is established, punishment will follow – anything ranging from a fixed penalty 'on the spot' fine to a fine in a magistrates court or even, potentially, imprisonment in a crown court. Drivers of motor vehicles are much more likely to be the subject of criminal prosecutions than cyclists, although there are some specific criminal penalties that apply to cyclists (see page 114).

Bikes are subject to many of the rules laid down in the Highway Code, which all cyclists should read – not just the cycling sections, but the chapters on general road behaviour such as road positioning. Stick to the Highway Code and you are more likely to be in the right in civil proceedings and anyone you are in collision with is more likely to be found guilty of a criminal offence, thus strengthening your case.

The final decision about whether and who to prosecute in Britain lies with the police and Crown Prosecution. Criminal Road Traffic legislation generally applies to Scotland as it does in England and Wales. Civil cases are governed by separate case law and for accidents in Scotland you may need to go through Scottish courts and need a Scottish lawyer.

Who pays – insurance

There is at present no legal requirement for cyclists to take out insurance cover as road users. However, if you hit someone and you are sued you may well wish you had taken out insurance. Third party insurance will cover you for any damage to other people and their property that is caused by you. Cyclists' Touring Club membership (see page 138) automatically entitles you to this cover and also gives you free legal advice in the event of an accident, so may be something worth thinking about. They can

even take your case on for you. If you are hit by a driver and the collision is their fault you can claim from their insurance. Irrespective of any such claim, you might also be able to claim from personal accident, travel, home or employer's insurance depending on the circumstances. State benefits such as Statutory Sick Pay may also be relevant. If you were deliberately hit by a driver either directly or with his vehicle you may be able to make a claim from the Criminal Injuries Compensation Board (even if the culprit isn't caught or prosecuted).

A case in point

Here are some sample cases, bear in mind that every case revolves around its own particular facts. There are no hard and fast rules – doubly so in civil cases.

1 Damages were awarded to a cyclist and against a van driver who was parked in a cycle lane. The van driver was judged to have put the cyclist at risk and to have disobeyed road traffic orders.

2 This case demonstrates the importance of standing up to unscrupulous insurance companies. A nine-year-old boy was knocked off his bike by a car while in a bus lane and suffered serious brain damage. The police refused to prosecute and the driver's insurers threatened to counter-sue. When the case came to court the boy won his claim. Most alarmingly the driver's insurers threatened to counter-sue the boy's parents and his childminder on the basis that the boy was not wearing a helmet and was allowed out unsupervised – despite the fact that he was simply exercising his legal right to cycle on the roads. The case was supported by the CTC's Cyclists' Defence Fund.

3 A cyclist sued the Highways Agency for their routing of a cycle lane in an allegedly torturous and dangerous manner around a bus stop. He hit another cyclist who was obscured by a stationary bus. It raises the issue of whether cycle lane design can ever be solely to blame for an accident or whether cyclists should take account of all

conditions. Certainly successful claims have been made against councils for damage caused from failure to repair potholes. Such cases rest on whether the council had a sufficiently good and regular system of inspection and are often difficult to predict. Judging whether a spill is your fault or the road's is more difficult than it may appear.

4 Don't automatically expect drivers convicted of what you would assume to be such serious offences as dangerous driving to get long prison sentences – they are often derisory, even if cyclists are killed as a result of their actions. In one such case a driver hit and killed a cyclist crossing a slip road and was sentenced to eight months in prison. Comment was made by judges as to the poorly lit nature of the road and the lack of reflective clothing of the cyclist as if to excuse that the main and proven fact of the case was the driver's dangerous behaviour.

5 Some accidents are not within the province of the law. One cyclist sustained damage after collision with a squirrel. Unfortunately for squirrel and cyclist, wild animals are generally outside the legal system. It's different with animals that are owned – a farmer was successfully claimed against over the behaviour of his geese, which strayed onto a road and caused a cyclist to come off. When there is no other party to claim against, personal accident injury may come into its own.

Criminal offences for cyclists

The following are criminal offences. Prosecutions are relatively rare – only 45 people were prosecuted for dangerous cycling in 1999.

- Dangerous cycling – riding so that 'it would be obvious to a competent and careful cyclist that riding in that way would be dangerous'. Maximum fine £2,500.
- Riding a bike without due care and attention or without reasonable consideration for others using the road. Maximum fine £1,000.
- Riding a cycle on a road or other public place when unfit to ride through drink or drugs. Maximum fine £1,000.
  Note: The police cannot demand a breath test or urine sample from cyclists so they have to rely on tests such as walking in a straight line to show you are unfit to control the vehicle.
- Pavement riding can now be punished with a fixed penalty notice of up to £20, payable within 28 days.
- Unauthorized road races and time trials.
- Carrying passengers, unless your bike has been specifically designed or modified to do so.

- You can take electric cycles on the road provided they don't weigh more than 40kg (88lb) are fitted with useable pedals and don't have a motor with an output of more than 0.2kw which is not capable of assisting the pedal at speeds of more than 25km/h (15mph).
- Failure to comply with traffic signs, failure to obey a traffic light and failure to give your name and address to a police officer when requested to do so.

Civil offences

- Riding on a footpath is not a criminal offence but a civil one and the landowner may sue you for trespass. Pushing a bike is a grey area but if you carry your bike along a footpath you are most likely not committing any offence because the bike isn't in contact with the path – useful to know if challenged and you want to get to the end of the path.
- If you ride negligently and cause physical damage or injury to another person or their property then you may be sued as described above.

The Highway Code will tell you what is expected from you and what you can expect from others as a road user. Be sure to know your traffic signs!

The Highway Code

The Highway Code has clear guidelines about how motorists should treat cyclists. It is not a legal document, but you should follow the general rules of the road laid down for all vehicles, excepting those rules that apply to prohibited roads (such as motorways). As with motorists, cyclists must obey all traffic signs and signals. The Highway Code also gives specific guidance to cyclists.

You must

- At night have front and rear lights lit, plus a red rear reflector and amber pedal reflectors if the bike was manufactured after October 1985.
- Ensure your brakes are efficient.
- When using segregated cyclist/pedestrian tracks you must keep to the cyclists' side of the track.
- Keep within cycle lanes wherever possible.
- Ride in single file on narrow or busy roads and not more than two abreast in any event.
- Keep both hands on the handlebars except when signalling or changing gear.
- Keep both feet on the pedals.
- On roundabouts either keep to the left or dismount and walk around.
- Bus lanes may be used by cyclists only if the signs include a cycle symbol. Watch out for people getting on or off a bus.

You must not

- Cycle on a pavement (of course this doesn't include newer style segregated pavements with cycle lanes painted on).
- Carry a passenger unless your bike has been adapted to do so.
- Ride under the influence of drink or drugs.

Drivers of motor vehicles should

- Give cyclists plenty of room when going past them or overtaking.
- Always look for cyclists when emerging from a junction or turning.
- Not park or drive in a cycle lane marked by a solid white line during its hours of operation.
- Not park or drive in a cycle lane marked by a broken white lane unless it is unavoidable.
- Not park in any cycle lane if waiting restrictions apply.
- Give way to cycle lane users when turning.
- Be aware cyclists may veer suddenly in high winds or on a road with many potholes.
- Not encroach on advance cyclists' stop lines at traffic lights, allowing cyclists time and space to move away when lights turn green.

First aid and injuries

Accidents do happen sometimes, so it makes sense to be prepared.

First aid

Many of us will either have witnessed, been involved in or will know of someone who has suffered a cycling accident. The number of cyclists killed in Britain in 2004 rose from 114 the previous year to 134, while the number of people seriously or slightly injured dropped, according to the Department for Transport. Put in perspective these figures are relatively low, however, it's vital that cyclists know what action to take if they're ever confronted with this sort of situation.

The first, most basic advice given by the St John Ambulance Service is to check for danger - the most likely for cyclists being whether or not to remove the person from the road. A casualty should not be moved if you suspect they may have a neck injury, but if they will be put in greater danger remaining where they are carefully move them to the nearest, safest place.

Once this is done, depending on the seriousness of the accident, call for an ambulance. Meanwhile there's a lot a trained first aider can do, starting with checking for ABC – that the Airways are clear, the Blood is circulating properly and for Consciousness. Determining these priorities helps you decide which injuries to deal with first.

C for consciousness is handled by talking to the person, which reassures them and allows you to access their level of response. 'If the person responds, but seems to be groggy then support them in a comfortable position and watch for changes. When the casualty has recovered make sure they're with a responsible person and tell them to go to hospital if they develop a headache, nausea, vomiting or excess sleepiness,' they recommend. The method for helping an unconscious casualty is taught on a St John's First Aid course.

It's always best to be prepared – with a few skills you could save someone's life. To find out about a St John Ambulance first aid course near you go to www.sja.org.uk/training or call 08700 104950

First aid kits

It is a good idea to have a first aid kit with you, for example if you are touring or mountain biking, but especially if you are riding with children.

There are a number of kits available which are tailored for cyclists, that are lightweight and easily portable. Remember, it is important to know how to use everything in your first aid kit beforehand. If you are putting your own kit together, you might want to consider the following items: elastic roll bandage; aspirin or ibuprofen; adhesive tape; alcohol swabs; antihistamine; antiseptic ointment; adhesive bandages, assorted sizes; gauze pads; hydrocortisone cream (soothes allergic skin); insect repellent; small mirror; cotton swabs; safety pins; scissors or Swiss Army knife; sunscreen; triangular bandage; tweezers.

Inspect the contents before every trip and make sure the tools are clean and supplies in good condition. Replace expired medicines and add items you wished you had brought on the last trip. Make sure the container is durable and waterproof, and stow it in an accessible place.

Cramps

Cramps generally occur when you use your muscles beyond their limit, which explains why they are more common at the end of a long or particularly strenuous ride. Make sure that your training is enough for the level of cycling you do, and that you have enough fluids with you as cramps are also caused by dehydration. To relieve the cramp, gently stretch the muscle. Calf cramps can be helped by standing on the bike and dropping your heel, while thigh cramps can be stretched out by moving your thigh backwards towards your buttocks.

Sprains and strains

A sprain is a stretch or tear of the ligaments. The symptoms are bruising and inflammation, normally accompanied by a tear or pop in the joint, depending on the severity of the injury. A strain is a twist, pull or tear of the muscles or tendons, leaving you with muscle spasm, weakness, inflammation or cramping. Both should be treated with rest, ice, a compress and elevation where possible. To avoid sprains and strains, build up your muscle strength, stretch regularly and warm up before strenuous cycling.

Heat stroke

Heat stroke is partly caused by dehydration (drinking alcohol can also contribute). It can develop very quickly and can cause unconsciousness within minutes. The blood is trying to cool the body down and is being taken away from the brain, which can make you feel sick. Try to cool off as quickly as possible. Ensure that you have plenty of liquid while cycling.

Cuts and scrapes

If you are unlucky enough to fall off your bike, clean any minor scrapes with mild soap and water or a mild antiseptic wash, and then cover the area with ointment and a dry dressing. If your injury is more serious, you can still help the healing process before seeing a doctor. Clean the area thoroughly and cover with a light dressing. Cuts that continue to bleed after fifteen minutes of direct pressure, or that go deep into the skin, may require stitches.

Boils

Big mileage racers may be more prone to boils, but you can still get them from commuting or riding shorter distances. Minimize the risk by using a saddle that suits your bottom and the clothing that you're wearing; and don't sit at your desk all day in your sweaty commuting clothes. Either ride to work and change, or ride slowly enough that you don't sweat. If you can't shower at the end of your commute, use a wet wipe on sweaty areas.

Knee pain

The most common cyclist's complaint. Some knee problems like swelling, clicking, or popping should be immediately seen by a doctor. Irritation under the kneecap can be caused by improper saddle height, or incorrect pedalling. If you ride in too high a gear or stand on the pedals this might make it worse. Shoes with ribbed soles that limit motion can cause pain if the knees, feet and pedals are misaligned.

Shin splints

Proper stretching can help prevent shin splints, and you can get supports for your leg to help treat the condition. The pain to either side of the leg bone may be related to a muscle imbalance. If you have collapsed arches you are more at risk of developing shin splints.

Achilles tendonitis

Not pedalling properly, riding with the wrong seat height, not warming up properly, or overtraining can cause inflammation of the tendon attached to the back of the heel bone. It is not normally a problem for beginners, but can be treated with ice, rest, aspirin, or anti-inflammatory medications. But if you have chronic pain, or swelling, go to the doctor.

Numbness

Small nerve branches between the toes when under pressure can cause swelling, leading to numbness, tingling, burning or sharp shooting pains. Try wider shoes or loosening the laces or toe straps. Another possibility is to try a riding without clips. Numbness or tingling with leg pain could be 'acute compartment syndrome', which is serious and requires immediate medical attention.

Exercise for new cyclists

Getting fit takes time, effort and commitment.

When you are new to cycling it all seems such a mystery: how can those riders go so fast? What do I need to do to get fitter? How do I build up my muscles? It's not easy to know what to do, and those around you – even seasoned riders – may not have the knowledge you're after. So whether you are starting afresh or coming back to the bike after time off, have patience, do the right things, and you will achieve a good level of fitness.

Starting out

At some time most of us start training. For some it might be after a lay-off through injury or illness, for others as part of a get fit regime. No one stays fit 365 days a year at 100 per cent of their potential, it's just not possible. So how do you get back on the road to fitness, or possibly help someone else to get into cycling? It's at this point, when you're starting out, that you are most likely to overdo things. Over training due to working too hard too soon (using the 'pain equals gain' philosophy) – rather than putting in a massive volume of cycling – can occur in just a few rides, resulting in pain and potential injury. The result is that you let the cycling go and lose what fitness gains you were making... so it's crucial that you do not do too much too soon and that you should ride steadily and slowly, building up your fitness. The fitness level you attain is a combination of your genetics, the time invested and the amount of correct training. It's not about who can go the hardest all the time.

Use your heart rate monitor to keep in the steady state or training zone.

1 Anaerobic warm-ups

After getting changed, putting your water bottles on and checking your bike, it's time to begin. The start of your ride is the vital part – it sets up the fuel use, your muscle co-ordination and your mental outlook for the rest of the ride. Common mistakes are to ride too many hills too soon, use big gears from the start or rush to get to work.

You should ride steadily and gradually, allowing your aerobic system to catch up with your increase in exertion – this can represent an increase from burning 80 calories/hour to 500–700 calories/hour. This takes at least 10 minutes, and ideally 15–20 minutes. So, choose the flattest route, give yourself time and start in easy gears. During every ride have a minimum of 10 minutes slowly raising your HR from 80–100 up to near to your aerobic maximum – or from easy leisure effort to breathing fully but in a controlled way. If you are in a hilly area, if possible use an indoor trainer for 10–15 minutes to warm up before riding outdoors. Get this wrong and you will: (1) cause lactic acid to surge into

Heart rate monitors

A heart rate monitor (HRM) is a recommended investment as it will enable you to maximize the effect of the training you are able to do.

The target heart rate during physical activity (walking and running as well as cycling) should be 60–90 per cent of the maximum heart rate. To calculate target heart rate, use the following formula:

1 220 (beats per minute) minus your age = maximum heart rate.
2 Maximum heart rate multiplied by percentage intensity = target heart rate.

A 40-year-old man would use the following calculation:

1 220 – 40 = 180 (maximum heart rate)
2 180 x 60% and 180 x 90% =108 to 162 (target heart rate)

your muscles, (2) use up muscle carbs you'll need later on, (3) put significant strain on 'cold' muscles causing micro-trauma injuries and (4) make the experience a misery. Start with a warm up – it makes sense.

2 Over-exertion workouts

If you can only ride two or three times a week then that's going to restrict your fitness progress and eventual maximum fitness level. The biggest mistake is riding too hard during the few hours you have to make up for not having more time. Don't. This is a big mistake as it creates an anaerobic overload, effectively you're 'over training' despite the fact you are on just a few hours a week.

The common psychology of this rider is: (1) I can't ride slowly (2) I'll never get any results at this level and (3) other riders ride this fast so why not me? If you work from home occasionally or can do a bit of flexi time, look at your time management to increase your riding time, frequency and your longest ride (see pages 120–123). You cannot ride above your aerobic maximum (70 per cent of heart rate reserve or 82 per cent of HR maximum) for more than a quarter of your training time. Ideally, at the start of your fitness building less than 10 per cent should be above this level. Stick with it, you will gain a rock solid fitness but at the pace of your genes. This is proven, elite athletes know it – it's a shame too many beginners think: 'I'll ride fast, do intervals, race a lot, which will make me fast'. It won't, you need months of building a base first.

Use your heart rate monitor to keep in the steady state zone – 180 minus your age – and not only will you reap more benefits, you will avoid burnout too.

Top tip

Remember, if you feel like it is too much hard work at first, just think how physical activity can increase your basal metabolic rate (resting rate) by approximately 10 per cent. This increase can last for up to 48 hours after finishing exercising, burning more calories for free.

3 Sweating it off

The majority of your sweating is caused by the heat you create when you cycle. Ride harder and you sweat more. Watch out for hotter days as they provide extra load on your body. In rides shorter than 45 minutes in cool conditions you can restore the fluids lost from sweating with a pint of water. But in rides over the hour in the heat of summer, indoors or even in winter, you'll lose 500ml (17floz) or more per hour. To maintain the correct electrolyte balance you should probably replace it with hypo- or isotonic-sports drinks. This fluid loss is not weight loss (fat loss will be around 20–50g/hr ($^3/_4$–$1^1/_2$ oz)) so you have to replace this lost fluid or your body's functions will be negatively affected.

You should drink a minimum of 500ml (17floz) of fluid replacement every hour you ride (150–200ml (5–7floz) every 15–20 minutes).

Time management

How do you achieve a cycling quality of life when your hours are filled up with work and family?

In a nutshell, by being clever with time, organized with equipment and using your opportunities to double up tasks and sneak in rides. Motivation plays a role too, so be prepared to sacrifice some lying-in and TV hours for extra time in the saddle.

Professional racers are the only group which have attained perfect control over their cycling hours. For the rest of us, no system is perfect. Many people become demoralized because they cannot ride as much they wish, or as much as they have in the past. So it is important to accept that slotting cycling into a busy week requires compromise in your standards. This particularly affects 30- and 40-year-olds, for example, who when they were younger perhaps rode at a high level, but now find themselves bound by the golden chains of career and children.

Relax your goals of speed and endurance to a realistic level, one you can maintain over a year, not just a week. Self-acceptance is extremely important if you are going to keep your identity as a rider. It is better to still be riding in 10 years' time at a regular level, than to have consigned your bike to the dustbin for no longer being top dog.

Riding flexi-time

Once you've accepted realistic goals, get clever with your time at home and at work to create slots and places to ride. You must use marginal times; early in the morning, journeying to work, lunch-hours and down-time at home. It takes effort and attention to get up earlier, keep kit together, resist the TV and another cup of coffee, but you're worth it. Aim to ride at least once a week, and preferably three to four times.

Early weekday mornings

While the day is young you are likely to be freshest mentally and physically, optimistic about the day and have the fewest demands on your time (parents excepted). Working-out early fits in well with washing, dressing and breakfasting – a doubling up of routines.

During the week, try going to bed half-an-hour earlier and get up at 7am rather than 7.30am to work out until 8am. Sounds stupid? Try it!

Commuting

The cyclist's classic training-for-free is the journey to work. Not everyone's job is a commutable distance and not everyone has storage and changing space at work, but you can vary your commuting and adapt around nominal facilities.

'No shower at work' is often quoted as a block, especially by bigger blokes. But in fact, if you shower before you leave home, the sweat is still pure (it is bacteria which makes sweat smelly, and that needs time to act); many people find once they have dried off, their colleagues suffer no aromatic ill-effects. Or at least try a strong deodorant before you quit!

The ideal scenario is a journey of 8–16km (5–10 miles) taking 30 to 60 minutes, which can be completed comfortably daily if you wish. Clear roads may be preferable, but even in the busy city centres, you can get a good flow going, and starting off from a dozen red lights is like doing sprint start reps. You may also find other cyclists to pace yourself against.

If your journey is less than ideal, adapt. If you have a long 50km (30 mile) ride to work, do it one way twice a week, alternating with the car or train. If you have a short 8km (5 mile) ride, invent a longer circuit, and use that extra early-morning half hour to double your usual distance. Don't feel you must ride every day; this allows for sickness, smart meetings and saying 'no' on wet mornings.

Leisure rider

Riding once a week is important, preferably would do more. The idea is to get out on a sunny day, keep up with the children, and maybe to do an annual charity ride. A personal goal could be to ride 30–50 kms (20–30 miles) to the coast every bank holiday, rather than go by car with the others.

Fitness rider

For fitness riders, who desire the health, looks and society of regular cycling, try not to drop below one big ride a week, and go for three rides when you can manage it – commuting is ideal for you, as is home training. Aim to complete a charity ride, or set yourself a long-distance trip with friends as a three-monthly goal. Every birthday try to ride the number of miles of your age!

Competitive rider

For racers, whose goal was constant improvement, the aim could now be to maintain a decent enough standard to stay competing. Race the guys around you rather than the leaders – they probably don't have as many demands on their time. Set a less challenging personal goal for timetrialling, and recognize achievement in hitting that. This may sound like a sell-out, but if you can stay fast enough to keep racing, you'll have achieved a sustainable balance between cycling and the demands of the rest of your life.

Lunch-time

Your lunch-hour is a golden time for pedalling. The issue is getting in and out of your kit, which takes 15 minutes a time, meaning that an hour yields a maximum of 30 minutes on the bike. You need to have your kit organized, and be content with a sandwich at your desk afterwards.

Because time is short, ride hard then really hit the gas on all rises or include intervals (short maximal efforts interspersed with recovery, such as sprinting to the next lamp-post, sprinting for two minutes, or doing hill reps). However, riding for longer than 45 minutes brings significantly more benefits. So if you can, take an hour and 15 minutes (perhaps by staying an extra 15 minutes at work?).

The ideal scenario is twice a week, say on Tuesday and Thursday. Combined cycle-commuting and lunch-time intervals give you around 90–120 minutes paced and maximal riding per chosen day without losing any family or relaxation time.

For leisure and fitness cyclists, 30 minutes riding at lunch-time may not merit the kitting-up time. To keep base fitness it is acceptable to walk, jog, do a gym class or swim. You get a full hour's activity, and, as all exercise is cumulative, an hour's walk on a Thursday will aid an hour's cycling on Saturday.

The home front

To keep travel and preparation to a minimum, work out near home as much as possible. At home, the ideal scenario is to have a cycle trainer (turbo) permanently set up somewhere for spontaneous half-hours as well as scheduled sessions.

Riding near home is another time-saver. Get your local Ordnance Survey Landranger map and chart the quiet roads and contours. Make up circuits a few kilometers/miles long that may not be scenically breathtaking but which use an hour efficiently. Ideally, you want something about 25 kms (15 miles) long (in total or circuits) with hills and flats. It may get dull, but the goal is effort and sweat, so put up with it.

Maximize your riding time.

Use bike shops to save prep time. Busy people are allowed to pay for simple maintenance even if they prefer to do it themselves; i.e. routine bike service, new brake pads, greasing cables.

Weekends and children

The waking hours, 7 a.m.–10 a.m., can turn into free workouts. Get up on Saturday or Sunday at your normal workday time and you can be back, washed and dried by 11 a.m., ready for shopping and the match.

This means no late nights Friday and Saturday!

If you are parents, exchange workouts with your partner or include them and the children in your training by getting the family to meet you somewhere on your circuit. Then you bask in their proud smiles – and they see a good role model.

Involve older children in your turbo-training (but keep little ones safely away from the whole whirring set-up). Get the child to time the session, to hold the stopwatch and shout commands, or even bang a drum for cadence! Use crèche facilities at local gyms where you can do weights, spin classes or swim, or put children into their own classes, e.g. junior tae kwondo. Share childcare with other cycling parents.

Cycle clubs based at cycle circuits and tracks may run junior sessions at the weekend, which allow you to train on the circuit simultaneously. Double up with other families with children – so everyone gets riding buddies.

Be organized

A lost shoe can mean two lost hill reps, so get a big box, boxes or a cupboard and segregate all your cycling kit there, so that within five minutes you can lay your hands on everything you need to ride.

The period when you get back home from a ride is critical in getting you out again soon. This is a weak point in the system, for you're likely to be tired and want to throw down the bike and ignore fixing chores. Wash clothing immediately or as soon as possible. Get the chain clean and lubed as a minimum. Leave a punctured tube out in the open for fixing and stashing as soon as possible.

Sample weeks for time-challenged riders

Leisure rider

GOAL: not putting on weight, enjoying the occasional gentle afternoon on the bike, or an easy charity ride.
WORK-OUT DURATION: up to 30 minutes.
WORK-OUT TYPE: walking, jogging or running, plus small bites of cumulative activity such as taking the stairs instead of the lift. Just get out of breath and sweaty.
FREQUENCY: three times a week (spread out to avoid injury), but no less than once a week.

Fitness rider

GOAL: maintaining fitness and weight, riding with other cyclists, occasional rides of two hours and over, an annual goal such as a touring holiday or organized challenge event such as a charity ride.
WORK-OUT DURATION: 30 minutes to one hour at least once a week, preferably three to four times a week; longer ride (around two hours) once a fortnight/every three weeks.
WORK-OUT TYPE: cycling on the home-trainer, commuting, lunch-time and weekends, also walking, jogging and spin sessions at the gym.

Competitive rider

GOAL: to stay racing
WORK-OUT DURATION: a minimum is weekdays 30 minutes to one hour at least three times a week, a longer ride every weekend, race at least monthly.
WORK-OUT TYPE: programmed twice-weekly workout on the home-trainer, paced commuting, maximal lunch-times and endurance/speed at weekends, spin classes at the gym.
NOTE: the key to staying racing is maintaining the speed and endurance you already have. Make a plan, don't miss a session and keep a diary.

Motivation

Sometimes it is hard to drag ourselves out of our armchairs and go for a ride. So what can you do to make yourself get out more regularly on your bike?

Motivators

- Get dressed in your cycling kit for fun – you can't stay at home after that.
- Visualize enjoying particular points on the ride.
- Plan something good to eat afterwards.
- Congratulate yourself that you've kept to schedule and can relax for a few days.
- Program work-out reminders into your computer or diary.
- Consider going on cycling holidays, or taking your bike on family holidays.
- Get the kids involved and you'll spend more time in the saddle.
- Keep a diary of your progress. Record your mileage, time, heart rate, mood and general diet and see how they improve over time.

Someone behind you

We all need a coach, but few of us have them. Although we might have a partner or close friend who is prepared to chase us into action, the feelings of spouses and partners have to be considered. But they can be good for nudging you out when you feel a lazy hour coming on. You can do the same for them. If your partner is getting miffed, buy them flowers to say thank you for filling in. It may be old-fashioned but it will be appreciated!

Team motivation and performance

For a team to reach its potential, each individual's priorities are vital. There are a series of steps that can be followed to assist teams in self-reflection and prioritization:

1 Work out the important questions. What do you want to ask the team to consider? They could be 'the performances of the team could be improved by...' or 'I would enjoy riding for this team more if...'. Others could refer to finances, sponsorship or perhaps the camaraderie. Choose the four or so most important questions for your team.

2 Each rider individually generates as many answers as they can to each of the questions in turn.

3 Each rider in turn feeds back their responses, only elaborating when clarification is needed. Now is not the time for discussion but for the construction of a master list of everyone's ideas.

4 Each rider then rates each of the ideas out of five, with five meaning of high importance and one meaning of little importance. Then all the scores are fed back. By adding all the responses together for each idea, the team is starting to get a team consensus of the ideas that appear to be the most highly thought of.

5 Agree an action plan to achieve the key ideas that have come out of the profiling exercise. For example, decide how the team leader will be decided upon, whether they will change in different races, and what happens if the team leader gets dropped?

Nutrition

Remember to take care of your body's energy requirements.

If you are riding a lot, drink concentrated fruit juice or specialist energy drinks. Your body will process the sugars and carbohydrates into the glucose that your cells can use. If you are aiming for say, two hours of intense riding you'll need plenty of carbohydrates which your body can convert directly into glycogen and store in your liver and muscles, whilst also keeping up your blood sugar levels. Without eating sensibly in preparation, your blood sugar will drop and you will become unable to maintain you're desired pace.

You'll need to consume a minimum of 250 calories per hour of fairly intensive riding. If you are trying to ride for longer by replacing the energy you are burning off it would be sensible to take in more. Fruits, particularly those that contain a reasonable level of carbohydrates such as bananas or nutrition bars, are ideal for this purpose. How much you'll need to eat to maintain your strength depends not only on the pace and distance you are trying to achieve but also on environmental factors. If you are riding hard on a consistently challenging terrain or cycling at high altitude you'll need to raise your glucose levels still further. For any strenuous ride though it's important to eat regularly and relatively frequently to avoid dramatic swings in your blood sugar levels.

Balancing your diet

Carbohydrates and sugars need to be topped up with protein and fat. You could try to follow the rule that suggests you should get 40 per cent of your calories from carbohydrates, 30 per cent from protein, and 30 per cent from fats, but it is perhaps more important to ensure that all you eat is easy to digest. In practice this means a little protein, some simple sugars, and lots of complex rather than refined carbohydrates.

It is also a good idea to have a small proportion of fat which can provide a much needed energy boost during longer rides, especially as an extra at normal mealtimes. Make sure though that it does not use up a lot of energy to digest. All in all, it is important to carry diverse types of food to be able to respond to all the dietary cravings you might experience, from 'sweet' carbohydrate-rich foods, to 'substantial' fatty snacks.

It is fine to eat while riding if your stomach can handle it, but be sure to wash the food down with the water your body needs to process it to prevent 'bloating', when your stomach sucks water out of the rest of your body. It's very uncomfortable, especially when riding. To get rid of bloating you'll need to drink plenty of water.

When to eat

Eat little and often. Don't over-eat at traditional mealtimes. Taking long lunch stops will leave you feeling sluggish in the afternoon and only impair your progress and enjoyment. Regular, light snacks are the key to feeling at your best for the whole of the day. At the other end of the spectrum you may experience a loss of appetite as a result of fatigue or sleep deprivation. Nonetheless you will need to eat so aim for 125-200 calories (2-5 biscuits or 1-2 bananas) each half-hour. Eating by the clock is the way to overcome a diminished appetite.

When preparing to begin your ride eat lots of pasta and high calorie, high carbohydrate foods before a run or a race. We only have reserves of 2000–3000 calories of glycogen, so the more we can replenish this the better. Try to avoid eating sugary foods immediately prior to a ride, as it will trigger an insulin reaction that will deprive your body of blood sugar, just when it needs it most. Instead aim to eat a decent and carefully balanced meal before you set off. It should incorporate lots of carbohydrates, perhaps pasta, protein in moderation and a small proportion of fats. Remember though to allow enough time for the meal to fully digest. It is a bad idea to eat a heavy meal within 2-4 hours of a big ride as you are sending your body mixed signals. Your body's resources will be sent to the leg muscles instead of the stomach, and the protein and fats will prove difficult to digest just when you need your body to begin the process of converting carbohydrates.

In the same way as it is unwise to eat a large meal before you set out, it is equally not sensible to feast when you've finished. Shortly after you stop you should eat around 400 calories from carbohydrates in order to begin to rebuild your muscle glycogen. Top this up with another 400 calories after a few hours' rest.

Riding for charity

Why not put your cycling skills to good use?

We all know that riding your bike can become quite addictive. That seems to be well understood by many charities, which is why they target cycling as a good way to raise funds. Many of the people who do charity rides are not everyday cyclists, but people who see riding a relatively long distance as a greater challenge than raising the necessary sponsorship money.

Charity rides are constantly evolving and more rides nowadays are aimed at race-fit or at least very well-prepared cyclists. At the most demanding end of the scale are rides such as 'Rome to the Dome' in aid of Leukaemia Busters, which covers 1,300 miles in two weeks, travelling from the ancient Coliseum to St Paul's Cathedral. The charity Action Research also hold an event called 'King of the Mountains Alpine Challenge', which takes in many classic Tour de France climbs for an intensive three-day event that tackles some serious gradients. If that's asking too much, don't worry, there is such a choice of rides available nowadays that there is something to suit everyone's level of fitness.

Broadening horizons

It is not just the hard rides that are attracting a new breed of charity rider but also the opportunity of a truly exotic holiday to places you might not otherwise ever get to visit. Organizers are increasingly appealing to people's adventurous nature and you can tour places like Vietnam, Mexico, Cambodia, Russia, Cuba and even Iceland, on well-organized events.

It is worth noting that the distances given in the details provided by charities/organizations, particularly of 'exotic' rides, can vary depending on the make-up of the group taking part. Many of these bigger foreign rides are a very attractive offer for participants who are prepared to put in the fund raising hours as well as the training hours. For these rides you will usually be expected to pay a 'registration' fee of a couple of hundred pounds, for which you can, for example, spend eight days riding along the River Nile, sleeping on a Nile cruiser and with use of the bike thrown in for good measure. Sounds too good to be true? For their

part the charity will ask you to raise a couple of thousand pounds in sponsorship money, which has to be collected before departure. Of the total you raise, it is usual for 40 per cent to pay for the balance of the trip and 60 per cent to be given to the charity.

Fitness questions...

If you have never ridden a charity event before then don't worry about not being able to make the grade... remember that charity rides are for your enjoyment and not a test of your fitness.

Most organizers have basic guidelines regarding your readiness for their particular event, and it is common policy for organizers to stop riders to regroup at regular intervals so the slower riders can catch up and therefore keep the group together and also give the event a 'cohesive' feel. To ensure the ride runs smoothly they will provide basic advice regarding the maintenance of your cycle prior to the event and also on the type of clothing and use of helmets, which while not compulsory, are strongly advisable. The organizers might give advice on the type of bike that's best but ultimately the choice is yours.

On long-haul trips many charities will even provide the bike (something like a 21-speed mountain bike) and that will, therefore, be clearly sufficient for the task. Most events, particularly the bigger ones, will provide good back-up services with a qualified mechanic in tow as well as water and food along the route. While organizers do everything they can to prevent rider burn-out, there is only so much they can do, and some (such as 'Rome to the Dome') require a medical questionnaire to be completed before you are even considered for registration.

Planning ahead

Because of the big miles and inherent logistical problems (booking accommodation, back-up, and so on) some rides have very limited numbers so getting in early for an event you like is very important as the cut-off date can be three or four months before the actual ride. For the bigger rides some charities recommend that you sign up six months in advance. In fact, Britain's biggest event, the London to Brighton, which attracts over 27,000 riders, has to turn entries away each year due to the high demand. This is partly because it is used by companies as a corporate 'hospitality' event for which they block-book places. If you can't get on the London to Brighton you could always try the British Heart Foundation's sister event, the London to Southend. These events are managed by a company called Cycle Rides (see page 138).

Although there is no definitive list available of all the charity rides taking place there is an organization called Challenges (Un)Limited, better known as Charity Challenge, who 'facilitate' events for charities. Due to the problems of organizing a ride, especially to somewhere like Iceland or Cambodia, Charity Challenge will take care of the logistical side. People can register for a particular event and then simply donate to the charity of their own choosing. Basically, they act as representatives for charity organizations and arrange events for over a thousand charities.

Although there are 'umbrella' charity watchdogs such as The Institute of Fundraising and the Charities Commission, they do not hold lists of events because, rather surprisingly, they do not legally need to be registered. In fact, anyone can set up a charity event. Some people do their own sponsored ride to raise the necessary money in order to enter another charity ride!

There is an 'unofficial' guide to organizing a charity ride available from the Institute of Fundraising, and members of the CTC can obtain their own guide on sponsored rides/charity rides (see page 138). Whatever sponsored ride you do you will find a great level of camaraderie amongst like-minded people. Once you've done an event (particularly a long one) you are likely to do it again. The Royal British Legion reckon 37 per cent of people return each year to their London to Paris ride. As the Marie Curie charity will tell you: 'every turn of the pedal does a good turn'. So get pedalling!

Touring holidays

How you tour depends on what kind of holiday you are after, your finances, motivation and aims. Here are three scenarios along with what you will need.

Credit card touring

Organized rides with sag-wagons may have popularized this form of lightweight touring, but it's also possible to do unsupported. The preconception of this type of touring is that it costs – well, you are buying what you need en route rather than carrying it. And credit cards inevitably conjure images of luxury – staying at the best hotels, which of course you can do, but you don't have to. The advantage here is the ability to ride fast and far – or just unencumbered. The disadvantage is that you have to be ruthless with your luggage because you won't be carrying panniers. Experience is the best teacher here.

Bike: Rack mounts aren't an issue as you won't be using them, but you will want a triple chainset to ease your knees on the hills. Minimal loads mean that sidepull brakes will be fine. Tyres should be at least 23mm, with 25, 28 or even 32mm preferable. Mudguards are optional in good weather. Suitable bikes include: any tourer; an Audax bike; or a road bike with a triple chainset.

Luggage: At the extreme you have what you stand up in, with your tools, race cape, credit card and energy bar in a large wedgepack. More practically, you'll want 10–15 litres of luggage space. On road, you could use a bar bag plus a large wedgepack. Alternatively there's the unfashionable but fantastically useful saddlebag. On road, the bar bag should be loaded with the lightest gear so as not to upset steering; off-road, you can use a wedgepack or saddlebag but not a bar bag. Light items can be carried in a small waterproof rucksack or hip pack.

Clothing: Wear clipless compatible shoes that you can walk in. Choose socks that provide rain protection. You'll either want two pairs of cycling shorts or a pair of touring shorts and two-plus pairs of underwear/short liners; you can wash them nightly. As well as a cycling shirt, you'll want a spare T-shirt, arm warmers, a race cape, and possibly a gilet. For evenings, lightweight poly-cotton trousers pack very small and light, plus you can wear them over your shorts if it's cold. Flip-flops or sandals are useful off the bike but are bulky.

Equipment: Lightweight multitool. Mini pump, two tyre levers, patches, spare inner tube, two water bottles, map(s), mobile phone, toiletries, sun block, plasters and pain killers. Your biggest burden will be your lock, which will weigh 1.5kg (3½lbs) or so if it's a tough one. Abus offer some lighter U-locks that still give reasonable protection. Cable locks are lighter but are easy to cut through. If you lose your bike your tour's over.

Accommodation: Unless you're camping, the choice is basically: Youth Hostels, B&Bs or motels/hotels. Youth Hostels are cheaper and always have a bike store, but meals are extra unless you bring your own and you have to be a member. B&Bs and hotels vary widely in price and quality. For a list of cyclist-friendly ones, get the Cyclists' Welcome pack from the CTC (see page 138).

Tip: Although you're travelling light, take a luxury item or two – a paperback, a handheld computer, a deck of cards, a small radio or an MP3 player.

Short-haul touring

If you want to carry more luggage, then short of a huge saddlebag, you'll need panniers. So you'll need a bike you can fit them to: probably a tourer, but possibly a hybrid or Audax bike. With larger loads, you'll want: lower gears (from a 22- or 24-tooth inner chainring), better brakes (cantilever or V-brakes), and wider tyres (32mm-plus). The extra capacity is good for a week or two's touring on the roads of Britain, Europe or North America – again, staying in hostels, motels or B&Bs – or for long weekends with autumn/winter clothing.

Bike: Ideally the frame needs rack eyes, however, if your bike doesn't have them – most modern mountain bikes don't – you can fit 'P' clips (available at good bike shops), and then attach racks to them. If you're using rear panniers, you need heel clearance for them and a frame that's stiff enough once they're on and loaded. All this points to a tourer. Wheels need to be 36-spoke, unless you opt for a 40-hole rear and 32-front. Although the tyres recommended for Credit Card Touring will serve, tougher tyres will stand up to more wear and tear. On a longer ride you're more likely to get wet, so use mudguards.

Luggage: Two panniers give you 25–50 litres of luggage capacity. Larger rear panniers are handy for shopping en route or carrying cast-off layers, but their disadvantage is that you WILL fill them, and putting that much weight there can upset the bike's handling. Two 'universal' panniers should be enough for one person.

Clothing and equipment: Same as for credit card couring, but more of it. You can afford to carry more 'luxuries' like spare sandals. You can also carry basic foods with you (tea bags, bread, cheese, etc.), which lets you take advantage of Youth Hostel kitchens. You can afford to take an SLR camera; padding inserts are available for bar bags.

Accommodation: Once again it's a straight choice between B&Bs and Youth Hostels. Or you could travel to a hotel abroad and use it as a fixed base for day-rides.

Tip: If travelling abroad, take photocopies of your passport and other important documents and store them separately from the originals in a waterproof bag.

Long-haul and expedition

An expedition can be anything from spending a few days cycle-camping in Scotland to a trip around the world. By carrying a tent and cooking gear you can be self sufficient, though the price of this will be a heavier load. This demands a sturdier bike, particularly if you're on rougher roads, far from bike shops. Reliability – and failing that, fixability – is your priority.

Bike: 26in wheels are stronger than 700c, and tyres to fit them are available worldwide. Use a width of at least 1¹/₂in (37mm), and take a spare, folded. Bar end shifters or downtube shifters offer greater reliability than combined brake/gear units.

Luggage: Racks made of steel tubing are stronger than those of alloy rod and are more easily repairable. If you're travelling far afield, get front and rear panniers. You may also want a bar bag and wedgepack. Take a spare pannier hook or two in case one snaps off. If you're travelling in Europe, you may manage with only two panniers with the tent on the rear rack. If you're camping with a mountain bike, you'll either want a custom rigid model with rack eyes, or a BOB Yak trailer.

Clothing: Clipless compatible shoes with a recessed cleat may split on a continent-crossing tour; platform pedals with toeclips, plus uncleated shoes, may work better. Clothes should be quick drying; avoid cotton. Take at least one complete change, preferably more. A heavier Gore-Tex jacket is better than a rain cape, and several thin layers beat one thick one. Warm on the bike is not warm enough off it. A good tight-knit woollen jumper or microfleece doubles as a pillow (rolled up).

Equipment: A proper first aid kit – and the skill to use it properly. Three or more waterbottles. In Europe, gas stoves are fine for cooking. Further abroad, a meths-burning Trangia or a petrol or paraffin-burning stove will be more dependable, but should not be used in the tent. Foods such as rice, pasta, noodles and oats are good bases for meals. As for tools, you need: 6 or 8in adjustable spanner, cone spanner, crank extractor, bottom bracket tools, headset spanner, spare spokes (rear wheel drive side are shorter, and will be the most likely to go) and a Pamir Hyper Cracker (removes cassette lockring and hence cassette to get access to

drive side hub flange for spoke replacement; Pamir's Cassette Cracker does the same for cassettes where the smallest sprocket screws on).

Accommodation: B&Bs and hostels for treats, otherwise your tent. A three-season tent and three-season sleeping bag plus a sleeping mat are essential for warmth and comfort. Reduce pack size by separating the tent and the poles/pegs. On no account put the pegs loose with the tent; it'll tear.

Tip: For illumination in the tent, or for finding your way back to it, an LED head torch is ideal.

Racing

Most road racing is carried out on the open roads but there are a growing number of races run on closed circuits

If you want to race then British Cycling and the League of Veteran Racing Cyclists are the main contacts. You may also be fortunate enough to have an active specialty group in your area, such as WOW (Women on Wheels). If you are under sixteen you may have to travel to find a juvenile category, while if you are over forty, the LVRC (League of Veteran Racing Cyclists), which run very informal road races for men and women, are particularly prominent in the East and North Midlands. Your local bike shop should have the contact numbers of local clubs but if they haven't, try your local library, council or newspaper or use the Internet. Don't give up or get frustrated if you find things difficult – cyclists often aren't that good at publicising themselves or the sport. The season will kick off around March and finishes around October time.

There are also quite a few good books but beware of the old-school attitude that more and more miles makes a better cyclist. This is fine if you have good base fitness and lots of time, but continuous illness and lack of energy can rob the enthusiasm of even the keenest beginner.

Categories

Once you become a Senior you can either amass points, or carry some across from your Junior racing to move up through the categories. All new Seniors start as a Fourth Cat and progress up through to First Cat and then on to Elite. Beyond this pro ranks beckon. Between the age of 18–22, riders race as Espoirs or under-23s as an introduction to Elite racing.
Woman: Any female over 18.
Youth: Categories are in two-year age bands – A under-16; B under-14; C under-12; D under-10.
Junior/Junior Woman: Under 18 but over 16.
Senior: Anyone over 18 years old and under 40.
Master: Anyone over 30 in five-year bands up to 70+ from Master A 30–34 to Master I 70+.
Private Member: Rider that is not a member of an affiliated club and rides without team-mates.
Primes: Pronounced 'preems', these are the prizes that award points, money or material to the first, or maybe

first three or more riders. Often held at the top of a hill or at the finish line on a circuit race, primes are designed to introduce spectacles.

Racing Etiquette

If you get in touch with a British Cycling coach via the BCHQ in advance of your first event, the transition into road racing will be much smoother. You may well hear a few bits of racing jargon or rules and etiquette referred to and it's important to get to grips with this as soon as possible.

Most road races start with a pep talk by the commissaire where things like sprint laps (primes) are announced or confirmed. The commissaire may also refer to the course risk assessment, which everyone has a duty to abide by, including the riders. Listen carefully to what is being said, because details of any changes will be hard to establish once the race has started. After this, it is over to what goes on in the bunch, which often comes down to who has enough breath to shout!

A shout of 'Huuuup!' generally means that a marked rider is just about to launch himself off the front. The usual response to this shout is for most of the bunch to start a chase, although this doesn't always happen, especially if unknown or weak riders are the ones launching the attack.

A shout of 'car down' or 'car up' means that a car is either approaching head on or coming up behind the bunch. Since most races will be on quiet roads, these warnings must be heeded in case of any danger.

Swinging off is when the lead rider leaves the front place of a group of riders. In a team time trial, or cooperating chase group, the lead rider will drop back on the windward side to protect riders going through to the front. Going through is taking up the lead position within the peleton (the mass of cyclists) or a smaller bunch of riders.

Through and off as the name implies is going through and then swinging off in one continuous movement. This is done when there are a large number of cooperating riders in a breakaway or chasing group.

Track race events

Whether you're a competitive cyclist already or not, track racing will have an event to suit your particular cycling strengths. Among the mains one are:

200m Time Trial: Typically used to establish seeding for the Matched Sprints, riders take a flying start, diving down from the top of turn two to the 200m start line, and then go all out to the finish.

500m Time Trial: Common track time trial distance for women and junior (15–16) men.

Devil Take the Hindmost: A mass start race, the rider who crosses the line last on sprint laps is pulled from the race. This continues until there are only a few riders left to sprint to the end.

Individual Pursuit: Riders start on opposite sides of the track, chasing each other for a given distance (typically 3,000m for juniors, 4,000m for seniors, 5,000m for pros), until one rider catches the other, or until the first rider finishes (fastest rider wins).

Keirin: The riders jockey for position (sometimes behind a single pacing motorbike) and jostle and jab each other with their elbows. The motorbike pulls off the track just before the last lap when the riders sprint to the finish line. Very popular in Japan.

Kilometre: From a standing start, a solo rider races against the clock. A test of speed and stamina in which each rider pushes himself to the utmost limits of his endurance.

Madison: Named after its place of origin, Madison Square Garden, New York. Teams of two or three riders compete, with the winners completing the most laps in an allotted time. After covering one or two laps at top speed, that rider drops out of the race so that another member of the team can come in and ride for a while.

Matched Sprints: Two to four riders race over a distance of 1km, but against each other rather than against the clock. Match sprints work by eliminating pairs of riders through heats. Only two riders compete in the finals, which consist of three races. The rider winning two of three final sprints wins the match.

Olympic Sprint: Three sprinters start the race on each side of the track, similar to Team Pursuit, quickly initiating a paceline. Unlike Team Pursuit, there are no exchanges. The lead rider leads the first lap, then pulls off; the second rider then leads out the second lap. After the second rider pulls off, it's up to the third and final rider to go all out to the finish. Somewhat misnamed, it's just now becoming an Olympic event.

Scratch Race: Riders start together, and the winner is the first to cross the line after a set number of laps.

Points Race: A variation on the scratch race, riders sprint for points every five laps (or so). The winner is the rider that accumulates the greatest number of points, not necessarily the first rider across the finish line.

Team Pursuit: Similar to the Individual Pursuit, but with a team of four riders on each side. Very exciting to watch and very fast.

Unknown Distance: A variant on the scratch race, except the number of laps is kept hidden from the field until the last lap, so no one knows when the end will be.

Omnium: Points are awarded to riders for their finishing positions in various race events throughout a meet. The greatest number of points is the omnium winner.

Where to ride

Not sure where to go? There are places to cycle all over the world...

Where to ride in the UK

You may think that as Britain becomes ever more packed with cars that there's nowhere left to ride. But you'd be wrong. Within the crowded shores there is a massive variety of cycling resources – city streets, rural roads, canal towpaths, dedicated bikepaths, byways, lanes, not forgetting some great off-road rides as well...

Linking the whole of Britain is the 16,000km/ 10,000 mile National Cycle Network. This is great for experienced and new cyclists, with a third of its route free of traffic. As it is a resource that is often shared with walkers, you still have to take care and bear their needs in mind.

The NCN is coordinated by the charity Sustrans in partnership with hundreds of organizations. It's not just for leisure riding either, but in places can provide your ride to work or school. Maps of the NCN are available from Sustrans, as is an official guide book.

On a similar note, the 6,400km/4,000 mile National Byway is a leisure-oriented cycling route based on quiet country lanes. The route concentrates on national heritage sites – prehistoric, geographic, historic, rural, industrial and social – and is an attempt at a sustainable development. National Byway area maps are available (see page 138).

If you are a keen mountain biker, Welsh trails are among some of the best-regarded in the world. There is also world-class off-roading to be had in Scotland and many fine routes in places like the Lake District, Quantocks and in many of the forests around UK cities. There are always some trails to hit...

Route planning

The most direct route may not be the quickest or most pleasant. While you're not taking in the sights like a tourer, it still helps to avoid heavy traffic, dangerous junctions or unnecessary hills.

Some enlightened councils publish cycling maps of their cities; ask at the local Tourist Information Centre. If they don't, CycleCity Guides have cycling maps for a number of towns and cities, including Birmingham, Bradford, Bristol & Bath, Glasgow, Leeds, Leicester, Central London, North West London, West London, Greater Manchester, Oxford, Rotherham, and Tyneside. A good cycling map can turn a nerve-jangling ride into an enjoyable experience.

For a rural commute, study a 1:25,000 or 1:50,000 Ordnance Survey map. The key to getting to work is to maintain a good average speed, not a good top speed. Back streets without traffic lights may be faster than a main road. A section of cycle path or tow-path, or even a bit where you have to get off and walk, may still save time.

Riding in Europe

From the generally flat landscapes of the Low Countries and the historic trail following the Danube River, to challenging Alpine terrain and the gruelling stages of the Tour de France, Europe has much to offer the recreational cyclist, the intensive mountain biker and the serious rider. Holland is perhaps the most cycle-friendly country. Its 16 million people own approximately 13 million bicycles and cycling is the

prevalent mode of transportation in its cities. In addition to this, the excellent network of designated cycle paths and routes that covers around 15,000km, its temperate climate and wide-open spaces make Holland a very practical destination.

A European cycle tour can be an effective way to see the continent on a budget, escape from the bustle of the cities and discover lesser-known destinations. Tours can either be 'fixed centre', where riders return to a base at the end of each day or 'moving on', a trip which can involve carrying your own luggage. Many travel operators offer fully supported cycling holidays on the Continent, catering for all ages, abilities and levels of fitness. For an example of some tailor-made cycling holidays see www.cyclingholidays.org and check advertisements in the cycling press.

If travelling independently, it is important to get your bike checked thoroughly for any problems, research your route with up-to-date maps and make accommodation plans before you depart. The official tourism website of any European country will normally include valuable information for those seeking to explore the country by bike.

Riding in the USA

America may be a country more associated with wide highways and gas guzzling vehicles yet there are over 57 million cyclists and cycling is an ideal way to explore the landscapes and history of this huge and diverse country. The Adventure Cycling Association (www.adventurecycling.org) is an invaluable source of information and inspiration, providing details of popular routes including the rides around the Great Lakes and the Grand Canyon. The ACA's Routes and Mapping Department have carefully built up a database of rural and low-traffic routes through some of America's most awe-inspiring terrain. This route network, selected, designed and mapped by cyclists for cyclists, was inaugurated in 1976 as the TransAmerica Bicycle Trail. Since then, the network has expanded to cover over 33,000 miles.

Cycling in America has a rich history. Founded in 1880, the League of American Wheelmen campaigned for protection from wagon drivers and horsemen as well as improved riding conditions, so they might better enjoy their newly discovered sport. Over 100,000 cyclists from across the United States joined the league to advocate for paved roads, an effort which ultimately led to the formation of the national highway system. Now known as the League of American Bicyclists (www.bikeleague.org), the organization continues to campaign for community cycling today.

America is also offered as a destination for many dedicated cycling holidays.

Riding worldwide

A cycling trip to raise money and awareness is a fantastic way of helping your chosen charity as well as seeing the world, for example riding along the Great Wall of China, from Saigon to Ankor Wat and the Andes to the Amazon. Travelling in small, fully supported groups, the only requirement is that you raise the minimum sponsorship level (which is usually set by the charity or organization involved). You can expect to receive ideas for fundraising as well as a guide to training that should help you achieve the necessary fitness levels before you depart.

Resources

Organizations to help you on your way.

Adventure Cycling Association

The ACA can provide a wealth of information on cycling in the USA. See www.adventurecycling.org

Association of Cycle Traders

With over 80 years' experience, the ACT provides an essential guide to independent bicycle retailers across the country. See www.act-bicycles.com

Bikeline Cycle and Motorcycle Accident Claims

Founded in 1998, Bikeline is a no win, no fee legal firm that specializes in representing both cyclists and motorcyclists in personal injury and accident claims. See www.bikeline.co.uk for more details.

British Cycling

British Cycling is the internationally recognized governing body of cycling in the UK. The organization is also committed to broadening the base of participation in leisure cycling in the UK. For further details see www.britishcycling.org.uk

Charity Challenge

The UK's leading adventure travel company is dedicated to inspirational fundraising expeditions across the world. They are involved in over 100 expeditions per year, helping over 2,200 participants raise money for the charities of their choice. Since its foundation in 1999, over £15 million pounds has been raised and over 550 charities have been beneficiaries. To find out about upcoming expeditions, including dedicated cycling trips, visit www.charitychallenge.com

CyTech

CyTech is the industry recognised standard for cycle mechanics. Established through ACT, the code is endorsed by suppliers and manufacturers as a benchmark of skills and services within bicycle retail. CyTech also offers training & accreditation opportunities both for those already employed within the bike industry and members of the public wishing to develop their cycle maintenance skills. Details of these courses are listed on the main ACT website, above.

Cycle City Guides

Cycle City Guides can provide detailed cycling maps for a number of towns and cities. To access their cycle maps database online visit www.cyclecityguides.co.uk

Cycle Rides Ltd

These are the people who manage the popular annual London to Brighton Bike Ride on behalf of the British Heart Foundation. See www.cyclerides.co.uk

Cycle Scheme

A great source of information on a cycle to work tax benefit scheme that makes a cycle commute an even more attractive option. The Government's Green Transport Plan enables employees to effectively lease a bike off their employer, exempt of Income Tax, National Insurance and VAT. Full details can be found at www.cyclescheme.co.uk

Cycle Training UK

A co-operative organization, Cycle Training UK is the biggest independent provider of on-road cycle training and cycle maintenance in Greater London. They also train instructors across the UK. Their website contains full details of their work and current courses, www.cycletraining.co.uk

Cycling Holidays

Whilst there are many companies who offer tailor-made cycling trips, www.cyclingholidays.org is the holiday and touring arm of the CTC. They offer a comprehensive range of trips all-year round. From weekend breaks in the UK to a challenging three-week tour in Myanmar there is something to suit all abilities and any budget.

Cyclists' Touring Club

CTC is the UK and Ireland's largest and longest established national cycling membership organization. In 2003 CTC celebrated 125 years of working for recreational and utility cyclists. They can offer advice on cycle training courses in your area. Call 0870 607 0415 or visit www.ctc.org.uk

The Highway Code

First published in 1931, the Highway Code is the official road safety manual for the United Kingdom and contains invaluable information for all road users, including cyclists. See www.highwaycode.gov.uk for more information.

Insurers

Always check the small print in your policy carefully but here are four companies that cover theft, damage and malicious damage cover.

CYCLECOVER is the insurance policy endorsed by the CTC. See www.butterworthinsurance.co.uk
BRITISH CYCLING – Evans Cycling Policy. Operated through E&L. See www.evanscycles.com
CYCLEGUARD is a service designed specifically for cyclists operated by Pavilion Insurance Management Ltd. See www.cycleguard.co.uk
CHURCHILL is a high-street insurance company that offers bicycle cover as an addition to your home contents insurance. See www.churchill.com

The League of Veteran Racing Cyclists

The League of Veteran Racing Cyclists provides a programme of competitive and social cycling events across the UK for men and women over 40 years of age. Their 2006 handbook can be found by visiting www.lvrc.org/hbook.pdf

London Cycling Campaign

The LCC is dedicated to making London a world-class cycling city. They provide a wealth of information on cycling in the city and actively support campaigns to promote cycling initiatives across the capital. Those who join the LCC receive a bi-monthly magazine and discounts at some bike retailers. See www.lcc.org.uk

The National Byway

The National Byway is a 4,000 mile (6,436 km) signposted leisure cycle round Britain. Designed to incorporate quiet roads and rural lanes, the route also incorporates over 1,000 places of interest along the way. Their website, www.thenationalbyway.org, outlines the initiative and provides the opportunity to purchase maps of the Byway.

National Transport Survey

The NTS is the only comprehensive national source of travel information for Great Britain that links different kinds of travel with the characteristics of travellers and their families. Their cycling specific reports can be accessed online at www.statistics.gov.uk

Police

Always report a theft to the police. You could help more resources be directed towards tackling cycle theft and even get your bike back. Either telephone or visit the local police station in person. You can even report online at www.online.police.uk

St John Amublance

St John Ambulance service provides basic first aid training across the country. For details of a course near you call 08700 104950 or visit www.sja.org.uk/training.

Sold Secure

An independent non-profit making organization administered by the Master Locksmiths Association which tests locks and certifies them. There are three levels of Sold Secure rating: gold, silver and bronze, which denote the length of time a lock will hold out against escalating levels of attack.

Sustrans National Cycle Network

A civil engineering charity which designs and builds routes for cyclists, walkers and people with disabilities. See www.sustrans.org.uk for details of cycle routes where you live.

Resources

If you were wondering about the makes, models, manufacturers or suppliers of the products shown, look no further.

Many of the products featured in the book have been recommended in Cycling Plus magazine. Please contact the manufacturers or suppliers to check out any new, improved or updated models.

10 (top) Squire Paramount, a high quality lock. www.evanscycles.com

10 (bottom) The front half of the Cateye HL EL-300 TL-AU100 Light Set. Provides value and performance, reliable, simple and quick to fit. www.cateye.com

11 The traditional Carradice Nelson saddle bag. www.carradice.co.uk

14 Adventure AT2 trailer with optional Stroller kit. www.ultimatepursuits.co.uk

16 Adventure F1 folding trailer bike. www.ultimatepursuits.co.uk

20 (TOP) Topeak Alien XS super compact multi function tool is the ideal touring companion. www.topeak.com

20 (BOTTOM) Topeak MTX Beam Rack & Side Frame. Beam rack with dedicated baggage that has moulded ribs that slide onto the rack, for day rides and light tours. www.topeak.com

48 Bell Metro helmet with winter accessories. www.thebellstore.com

49 AS NUMBERED:
(1) Bell Bella 2. Good value multi-purpose helmet with good retention system and airflow. www.ultimatepursuits.co.uk
(2) Limar 911. Comfortable and great value, with 37 vents and a removable visor. www.jimwalker.co.uk
(3) Diamond Back X-Treme. A good quality and good looking budget helmet. www.raleigh.co.uk
(4) Specialized Chamonix-R. Well-priced with in-moulding. www.specialized.com
(5) Specialized Air Force. A great beginner's helmet with loads of style and good safety features. www.specialized.com
(6) Casco Vautron. A protective design and TUV make this a safe bet if you like the looks. www.fine-adc.com

50 Decathlon Sport 100. Sizing small and compact, deal for women's heads. For recreation or occasional biking, great value for beginners. www.decathlon.co.uk

52 (TOP) Smart rechargeable LED, good for being visible, convenient and easy to use and charge. www.fisheroutdoor.co.uk

52 (BOTTOM) S-sun Focus Lamp, rear red, packs a lot of light for a little lamp, very well made. www.s-sun.com.tw

53 Dynosys Lightspin. This dynamo's patented magnetic arrangement offers very little drag. www.gearshift.co.uk

54 Magnum Ultimate. One of the best U-locks around.

55 AXA Ferrox 18012C. Not the strongest lock around, but at 1.8 metres the length is a bonus. www.amba-marketing.com

56 (TOP) Onguard 5019 Chain. A metre-long chain with 12mm diamater links and reasonably secure. www.moorelarge.co.uk

56 (CENTRE) Masterlock 4605D. Not a high security device, but useful for very short stops. (no website).

56 (BOTTOM) Onguard 3001. A low-priced lock, not too bad for the money, but not the tightest security around. www.moorelarge.co.uk

59 AS NUMBERED:
(1) BBB Rainwarrior. These functional guards to an average job for an excellent price. Greyville: 0543 251328
(2) Dirt Monkey. An off-road model intended for 26in or 20in wheels. www.halfords.com
(3) Topeak RX Defender rear. A plastic, seatpost-mounting guard with a detachable 'tail', which screws on for extra length. www.extraux.co.uk
(4) PRO Race mudguard. Basic spray protection for a road bike. www.bikeplus.co.uk

60 (TOP) Truflo Micro CO2 mini pump. www.truflo.com

60 (CENTRE) Park Rescue tool. www.parktool.com

60 (BOTTOM) Blackburn Mountain mini pump. www.blackburndesign.com

62 The Copilot Limo. See www.cyclesurgery.com

63 (LEFT) Hamax Sleepy. Easy to fit and reasonably comfortable. www.fisheroutdoor.co.uk

63 (RIGHT) Centric-Safe Haven. Good for balance but less good for pedalling, so best suited to shorter trips or off-road. www.phatbritain.co.uk

67 Ortleib Bikepacker Classic. Favoured by commuters and expedition riders alike. www.ortleib.com

75 AS NUMBERED:

(1) Hind the Basis. An ultra thin, sleeveless vest, ideal for warm, wet winter weather. 01424 753566

(2) Assos Airjack. Good fitting and performing kit. www.assos.com

(3) Cannondale Morph Womens. A well priced and versatile jacket-cum-gilet for all but the wettest of days. www.cannondale.com

(4) Foska Bones Hi-Vis. Highly visible at night, good fit. www.foska.com

(5) Helly Hanson V-Neck T. Designed to wear as a second skin. www.hellyhanson.com

(6) Altura Curve Women's Jersey. A cosy winter jersey with fleece lining – great value for money. www.zyro.eu.com

(7) Parrot Hydroline. Good all rounder, with good visibility. www.parrot-online.com

(8) Rapha Sportswool Jersey. A blend of merino wool and polyester – the resulting fabric has a feel like no other. www.rapha.cc

(9) Lusso Breathe Long Sleeve Polo. A fantastic value base layer, made from a microfibre fabric which is fleecy on the inside and has a smoothish outer. www.lusso.co.uk

77 AS NUMBERED:

(1) Agu Bikeboots. An easy way of keeping socks dry and shoes presentable. www.ultimatepursuits.co.uk

(2) Altura Cascade Trousers. For normal clothes commuting and steady touring, you'll want overtrousers. Fully featured and effective. www.zyro.eu.com

(3) Pearl Izum Cyclone Women's Gloves. Well fitting winter gloves. www.minx-girl.com

(4) Adidas Climaproof Overshoes. Good looking and performing reflective winter overshoes. www.chickencycles.co.uk

(5) Endura Thermolite Bib Longs. Great all round thermals. www.endural.co.uk

81 AS NUMBERED:

(1) Gill Rapide Windbrake Smock. High performance and great for all-year mountain biking. www.gillbike.com

(2) Sugoi Iron Narrow Tank. Comfortable and supportive for on and off the bike use. www.sugoi.ca

(3) Corinne Dennis Colorado. Technical fabric suitable for serious use. www.corinnedennis.co.uk

(4) Lusso Meat & Two Veg. Long baggies for singletrack or beach cruising, not touring or commuting. www.lusso.co.uk

(5) Campagnolo Raytech. Comfortable bibshorts. www.jimwalker.co.uk

(6) Hind Sidewinder. Simple styling for a women's short. www.hindclothing.co.uk

(7) Shoes by Time. www.time-sport.com

(8) Shoes by Shimano. http://cycle.shimano-eu.com

(9) Shoes by Carnac. See www.totalcycling.com

(10) Polaris cool mitts. www.polaris-apparel.co.uk

92 Datatool Fortress 1 Ground Anchor. www.datatool.co.uk

93 (TOP) Onguard Boxer 5046 Padlock. 01332 274200

93 (BOTTOM) Micromark Shed Alarm. www.mircomark.com

Glossary

If you need to become familiar with cycling terms, this is the perfect place to start.

Ankling
The practice of lifting and dropping your heel whilst pedalling.

The 'bonk'
Fatigue resulting from muscle glycogen depletion usually developing between one and two hours into a ride. Always carry a high energy snack to avoid it.

Cable locks
Portable, light, flexible and reasonably priced, cable locks provide an effective visual deterrent but they are perhaps best used as a secondary security device.

Chain locks
Heavier, though more secure than a cable lock. Its strength is determined by the type of steel used.

City bike
Stripped down mountain bikes for city streets.

Clipless pedals
Clipless refers to not using an external toe clip. They require a special cycling shoe with a cleat fitted to the sole, which interfaces with a locking mechanism on the pedal which means that you can pull the pedals up as well as push down.

Cordura
Light nylon material often used for pannier bags.

Cotton Duck
A super hard wearing, easy to repair material used for panniers. It is, however, only 95 per cent waterproof.

Derailleurs
A mechanism for moving the chain from one sprocket to another to change gears on a multi-speed bicycle.

Drop bars
Handlebars commonly seen on all racing bikes and most touring bikes, they allow a variety of hand positions.

Dynamos
Lighting system that employs a roller wheel driven by one of the bike's wheels to provide lighting power without batteries. Not as popular as they once were on account of the drag they cause.

Folding bike
Ideal if your commute involves other modes of transport as well. Great for short urban journeys.

Forks
Usually refers to the front fork, the part of the frame set that holds the front wheel. The fork is attached to the main frame by the headset. The fork consists of the two blades that go down to hold the axle, the fork crown, and the steerer.

Gore-tex™
An industry standard, the structure of the fabric forms an effective barrier against wind and rain, while still allowing water vapour to pass through. This helps to keep the wearer warm and dry, while the breathability allows sweat to escape.

Ground/wall anchors
These provide a fixed point to lock your bike to and are ideal for home security i.e. garages and sheds with solid (brick/concrete) walls or floors. The perfect companion to a good quality chain lock.

Headset
The bearing assembly that connects the front fork to the frame, and permits the fork to turn for steering and balancing.

Hybrid bike
Exactly as the name suggests: a hybrid of a road bike (700c wheels) and a mountain bike (frame .

Immobilizers
Alarm system that sounds as soon as the circuit, a loop of wire around the bike, is broken. For very short term use only.

Indexed shifting
Indexed shifting means that the shift control has click stops that provide discrete positions corresponding to different gears.

Kick stands/propstands
As there is almost always something for you to lean your bike against, carrying a stand around means extra weight for little advantage.

Peleton
A French term used to describe a mass of moving cyclists.

Recumbent bike
A distinctive looking bike on which the rider sits on a seat or hammock and pushes the drive with legs closer to the horizontal than vertical.

Roof-mounted racks
These fit to standard roof bars. You'll need one rack per bike and factor in the cost of a set of bars.

Seatpin
The hollow tube that connects your saddle with the frame. Usually aluminium or if expensive, carbon fibre, it allows adjustment of saddle height.

Shackle locks
Also known as a 'D-lock' or a 'U-lock' because of the distinctive shape of its rounded bar, the shackle lock is one of the most secure types of lock on the market. However, by being made of hardened steel, it is not the easiest to carry around.

Sprocket (front or rear)
A toothed wheel or gear that is part of a chain drive.

Steerer
The steerer, or "steering column" is the upper part of a front fork, to which the handlebar stem and the turning parts of the headset attach.

Stem
The part that connects the handlebars to the steerer of the fork.

Strap-mounted racks
Simple racks that rest against the back of a vehicle and are attached by a strap.

Suspension seatpost
These can be used simply as a way for recreational riders to alleviate some discomfort, or as a performance upgrade for increased climbing and cornering traction, and reduced fatigue.

Toe clearance
A measurement usesd to prevent the likelihood of your shoe hitting the front wheel when turning sharply.

Touring bike
Long distance load luggers built for comfort and strength.

Towball/towbar mounted racks
These racks mount the bikes low down on the back of a vehicle. This causes less wind resistance, thus reducing fuel consumption. Low racks can often obstruct the lights and number plate so you'll need a lighting board together with lights as well.

Tribars
Only usually found on time trial bikes, they engage the rider to use the aero qualities of a downhill skier for extra speed.

Tyre clearance
The distance between tyre and mudguard. A gap of 10mm ($^1/_3$in) is recommended.

Cycling Plus is Britain's leading monthly road cycling magazine. Visit www.cyclingplus.co.uk

Contributors

The publishers would like to thank the following Cycling Plus writers for contributing to this book:

Joe Beer
Nicky Crowther
Patrick Field
Cass Gilbert
Richard Grigsby
Bex Hopkins

Dan Joyce
Rebecca Lack
Richard Peace
Paul Smith
Hilary Stone
Andy Waterman

Thanks also to the Cyclists' Touring Club for the information on page 98.

Picture Credits

All pictures are the copyright of Cycling Plus except for the following:

Dave Atkinson: 93 (bottom)
British Heart Foundation: 113, 128
Paul Carpentar: 22
Jonathan Gawler: 131–133
Cass Gilbert: 2, 19, 21, 46, 66, 69, 118
Justin Hunt: 23, 24, 37, 82, 105, 111, 115, 116
Dan Joyce: 63
Rebecca Lack: 40
Robert Morris: 95
Jason Patent: 91
Richard Peace: 96
RANS Bicycles Inc: 29 (bottom)
don jon red/Alamy: 5
Warren Rossiter: 38
Robert Smith Studios: 15, 17, 64, 101, 124, 125
Paul Smith : 9, 12, 48, 49, 50, 52, 54, 55, 56, 62, 77, 79, 92, 93 (top), 123, 126
Steve Thomas: 58
Sam Walker: 98

First published in the United Kingdom in 2006 by Weidenfeld & Nicolson
10 9 8 7 6 5 4 3 2 1

Cycling Plus is an imprint of Future Publishing, Beauforc Court, 30 Monmouth Street, Bath, Avon BA1 2BW

Design: Grade Design Consultants, London
Assistant designer: Justin Hunt
Edited by Claire Wedderburn-Maxwell
Research by Brónagh Woods

A CIP catalogue record for this book is available from the British Library

ISBN-13: 978 1 84188 263 5
ISBN-10: 1 841882 633 1

Printed and bound in Italy

Weidenfeld & Nicolson
The Orion Publishing Group Ltd
Orion House
5 Upper St Martin's Lane
London WC2H 5EA